*The Model ''Villa'' - North Gate*

# Walking In Tower Grove Park

## A Victorian Strolling Park

### Second Revised Edition

by

## Robert E. Knittel

and

## "Herb"

## Illustrations

by

## Daniel J. Weismann

GRASS-HOOPER PRESS

Second Revised Edition

International Standard Book Number: 0-933038-03-8 Paperbound
International Standard Book Number: 0-933038-05-4 Clothbound

Library of Congress Catalog Number: 83-82822

Published by:

Grass-Hooper Press
4030 Connecticut St.
St. Louis, Missouri  63116

Manufactured in the United States of America

Dedication . . .

To ''Herb''

Without his enthusiasm for walking, this book would not have been written.

'Herb'

# Contents

List of illustrations

List of architectural details

# Foreword

It should be clear from the outset that there is walking and then there is walking, strolling, ambling, watching. The first is a way of getting somewhere. The second is a means to no end. The means is the end. The art of the second is what I am concerned about.

Victorians understood the art. They created huge canvases, strolling parks, upon which individuals ambled in daily and seasonal patterns. The pathways, swards, and water sides formed a web that held countless personal rituals of walking.

The Japanese, apparently, still practice the art. Their parks are smaller, yet more intricate. They are really gardens in which slowness is a virtue. The rituals walked-out there are a blend of strolling and meditation; a study of beauty in which changing perspective brings the same joys that varying kaleidoscope patterns bring to children.

I write about this kind of walking to explain it, as an anthropologist might explain any curious ritual unfamiliar to the folks back home. I must, because it is so unfamiliar to most of us. Ask a friend who has driven to see you, what was seen on the way. The answer will be very short. Even a report on a long journey will be, most likely, a simple itinerary. You will hear place names, not what was seen, or heard, smelled, or touched. The same is true of one who exercises, who has run or walked with eyes fixed on a watch or the random objects that serve as guideposts and goals.

Perhaps children still experience walking, those who are fortunate enough to wend their way to school on foot or who haven't been mesmerized by television. Many of us recall a special intimacy we enjoyed with nature as children. It seldom occurs to us that this was so because we walked.

Few adults stroll. Very little is experienced between the human constructs of home, car, and workplace. Tragically, it leads many to conclude that there is really nothing to be seen. The result of this is all too evident. Neighborhoods are built with no walks. Parkways decay. Worse, in many large city areas, including parks, to stroll is to invite predation as a slow caribou attracts wolves. Thus the determined tunnel-visioned gait of city dwellers.

Happily, places to walk remain. There are places where private rituals can be wrought. They are places where personality can be bound with natural sights, sounds, smells, tastes, and touches. One must find these walks by walking. Over millions of years our senses have been fine tuned to that uniquely human pace. To walk is to experience with all of our senses, to integrate our being with that of the natural and human world. It is this sense of integration, re-lived every day, that brings joy. Joyous things must be told. A person who *must* tell you what has been experienced on foot has walked. That person must share, as my friend Robert Knittel shares in this book. Join him.

Mark Miller

# Preface to the Second Edition

When I wrote "Walking In Tower Grove Park" I had hoped to acquaint a few people with the magic and beauty of this St. Louis landmark. What I did not realize was that there are a large number of people who have already enjoyed its beauty and are still enjoying it. Some long to return to it, perhaps to a time when they were younger, when, as children, they played their happy hours away in the park's many secret places. The response to my wandering in the park, and on paper, has been tremendous and for that I am grateful.

It is because of this response that I have published a second, revised edition. Some changes have come about in the park, perhaps more change than in its previous history since completion. So I thought I should try to chronicle some of these, and add to the descriptions of the seasons from my store of material. The Winter season has been greatly expanded and you will find new things here and there in the other seasons as well. Dan Weismann, the book's illustrator, has kindly given us some more drawings of the park and its architecture for which I am also grateful. And I have Fred Houska to thank for taking more photographs from which the drawings could be made.

Other things change as well. Herb no longer walks the park with me, having gone to his own special park reward less than a year after the book was published. When I walk the park alone I am sure that I hear his four-legged gait in the rustling of the leaves, and his spirit in the whistling of the wind. For helping me find the special places in the park, off the beaten path, I owe him a debt of gratitude.

And my thanks to all of you who, like myself, measure the changes of your lives by the changes of your seasons in the park.

Robert E. Knittel
August 23, 1983

# Preface to the First Edition

For thirty years, off and on, I have lived near Tower Grove Park, about three blocks away. During that time I visited the park often, usually driving through or walking along the paths. But I really began to know the park and see its beauty when I started to walk there with my dog, Herb.

Herb did not care for paths. He liked to chase squirrels, and birds, and to hunt moles. Since I always had Herb on a leash, I naturally followed him whenever he indulged his whims. So, in effect, Herb began to take me for walks, and it was then that I learned of the great beauty of the park.

Tower Grove Park is a strolling park, and was designed that way by Henry Shaw and his associates. Although some may come to play ball or tennis, or just picnic, the true beauty and genius of the park is realized through walking it, not only along the paths, but just walking wherever your fancy takes you.

What I have attempted in this walking guide to Tower Grove Park is not a sightseeing guide to the monuments and buildings, nor a history of the park. Rather it is an attempt to lead you along ways I have walked in the park with Herb, my dog. And you may see the same things we have seen driving the roads or walking the paths, but from a different perspective and, perhaps, a different mood. For the pleasures of walking are not only in the changes of perception and visual stimulation that walking provides at a human pace, but it is also the time it provides for thinking and reflecting, for being alone with oneself and with nature.

This book is written not only for those who are ambulatory, but for those who, for one reason or another, cannot walk or cannot see, and also for those who cannot be here, in the park, although they would like to walk it.

The book is in two parts: a walking guide and the seasons in the park. The guide consists of three walks, which will take you from one end of the park to the other, but each of which can be walked within twenty to thirty minutes at the least. The time will depend on the walker and the seeing that one wants to do. However, on those three walks you will not see it all, and much is left to your own exploration.

Perhaps the most important part of the guide is the five sections describing my meanderings with Herb, and personal impressions in the park during various times of the year, Early Spring, Late Spring, Summer, Autumn, and Winter. These seasonal sections attempt to give a picture of what walking in the park might be like, and what you might encounter, at different times of the year.

Herb and I hope that you will enjoy the walking guide as much as we enjoy walking in the park.

Robert E. Knittel
October 16, 1978

*Gazebo near lily ponds*

# A Very Special Place

*"Mr. Shaw's idea was to make Tower Grove Park
a place where little children might play, and work-
weary folk might rest, a place of worship among
the trees where tried souls might come nearer to
God."—James Gurney*

In the words above, James Gurney, chief planner and planter of both Tower Grove Park and Missouri Botanical Garden, described Henry Shaw's dream of creating an English strolling park, "a place of tranquility and ordered beauty." Shaw chose well when he brought Gurney from Kew Gardens in England to undertake the fulfillment of his dream. Gurney's idea of a city park was described as one "walled in by tall trees and shrubs so as to shut out the buildings, and give the impression of a great forest, where overstrained nerves, tired bodies and weary brains can find complete rest. With this idea in mind he planted trees and shrubs so that Tower Grove Park could be closed in with a wall of green. Every tree was placed where it is for a special effect."

Shaw and Gurney planted 20,000 trees on the three-tenths, by one and one-quarter mile strip of treeless farmland which comprised about 285 acres, all with an eye for detail and effect which is still alive when one walks the park today. Shaw had spent eight years touring Europe, observing parks and "pleasure grounds" in England, France, Germany and other countries. He examined the reports of park authorities in New York, Philadelphia, Boston and other large cities in the United States. Some of the designs were suggested by the book "Parks and Promenades of Paris." Ten gazeboes, those frail, almost ethereal canopies raised on slender columns and dripping with ornamentation, were built on European models under Shaw's direction.

1

Shaw and Gurney, together, created a very special place. Shaw, who came to St. Louis from Sheffeld, England in 1819, made his fortune selling hardware and retired at 39. They began the park in 1867 and completed the work in a few years with a $360,000 bond issue from the City of St. Louis. The park continued to receive gifts of statues and busts from Shaw, who had given the land to the city with the stipulation that he be director of the Board of Park Commissioners for his lifetime. From this position he designed and influenced the park's artistic completion.

That Tower Grove park is a very special place cannot be denied. Writings, letters, conversations with people in and out of the park, all attest to its unique and special nature. What makes it so? As with all special environments that tend to expand the soul, it has its own secrets. Perhaps the care with which each tree and shrub was placed, the lyrical structure of the gazeboes and music stand, the grand, expansive style of the gates and gate houses, the imposing presence of the statues, the quiet meditation of the ruins, pond and fountain, and the brooding towers over all, these together make of Tower Grove Park a very special place.

Whatever it is, people have felt it in the past and continue to feel it. And when they return, they feel it once again. I have walked the parks of many cities in Europe, South and Central America and the United States. Each has its charm and even majesty, but none can compare to Tower Grove Park in St. Louis. The charm is ageless, as attested by Harry Burke, writing, in 1923, a long and beautiful description of Tower Grove Park for the St. Louis Times. "Tower Grove is a spinster . . . Yes, she is one, I think, of the little old maids of the world. Reclusive, almost, in her sheltered home, freed from the anxieties of toil, permitted to withdraw from the tarnishing contacts of the mob. A spinster by vocation, keeping herself unspotted, and quaintly young, though with a perfume of other days about her."

I invite you to step inside with me, into the home of a very prim and proper lady, whose company you may enjoy daily, if you will only pay her a little attention.

2

# The Seasons In Tower Grove Park

*The Pretzel Man*

# The Park
# In Early Spring

*"Flowers and trees talk. Blessed is he who listens and heeds what they say."—James Gurney*

On a warming February morning, late in the month, but well before March, I walked with my dog, Herb, through the Roger Place entrance, as I do at least once a week. Walking aimlessly, having become used through the winter to seeing the bare trees and their unique shapes against the sky and land, and feeling it as just another winter day, I suddenly find myself underneath a tree looking at buds on the twigs, buds reaching down almost into my face, fuzzy little leafy buds. I reach up and touch the twig and the buds and now hold them in my hands and squeeze them softly, and feel the surging of Spring through my hand into my body. And then I look up anxiously at all the trees to see if they have yet shared in this tremendous event. They give no clue at a distance, but the birds sing, and the earth smells fresh and in the air is a promise. I look closely at the next tree, and it too has small unobtrusive bumps of budding buds. I go on, a Spring excitement all about me, glancing at every tree, holding some as I go by, feeling the freshness of their life pulsing once again through their veins. And I come then to another tree that is full of the fluffy buds which almost look like flowers and I wonder what they are. Looking at the buds I cannot tell, but I will know before the Spring is done. I will know them each and having seen their buds flesh out will watch the metamorphosis of greenery which adds such majesty to the park.

And here I come now to a tulip poplar, which has its flowers still dried from the Winter and awaits the casting off and the new promise. How glorious it is, after having walked the hard ground of Winter, to be able to walk on the soft ground and feel it yielding under your feet, the grass springing down before and then rising up behind. It is a feeling of Life.

But my dog Herb knows no season and hunts relentlessly, following the burrows of the moles which slope gently above the ground, digging them to their ends, unfortunately for the moles. Having crossed over from the statue of Alexander von Humboldt, I suddenly look up, as if signaled, and find that I am into the branches of a huge ginkgo tree, and see its limbs covered by smooth, round, bulbous warts. I had been looking forward to seeing the buds at this stage for some time, and I touch a large one firmly, and press it, and find it yielding with the sap that is flowing through it. And I gaze up to the fantastic lacework grill of the limbs and buds, and say to myself that this is a moment of Life that is with us always to transcend Death.

Looking to the right I see a great gum tree holding fast, still, the fruits of Winter, waiting patiently to cast them off with the new life of Spring, which will occur, no doubt, within a few weeks. And I mark the promise well, and hold it inside me.

Across the way I see the Music Stand and before it a tree laden with what appear to be red berries. And I rush now with Herb across the drive to see it more closely, and find that it too is one of the budding trees with almost blossom-like buds that I had seen on first entering the park. Only it is heavier and gives a color to the sky all its own. And I wonder as it nods to the statues of the musicians and composers, if it touches them too, and if there were not some connection in their lives, where they once touched the bud that gave a surge of life within, that found expression in their music.

Then going close to the Music Stand, I see, for the first time, a plaque on the corner, very unobtrusive, and it says, "Henry Shaw Music Stand, Erected 1872." And I think

6

that makes it over a hundred years old. And it goes on to say, "Repaired and restored in 1965 . . ." and lists the merchants and others who donated time and money to the project. And I think that it is fine that the local merchants have restored the Music Stand, and that their names are preserved in bronze for posterity.

The Osage orange trees, I can see, are not yet budding. Here is a young tree, planted recently, with red tips on the end of its branches, and it too has tiny buds emerging, more of the flowering red buds, all over now, a whole grove of them.

I approach now the pond, which is ice free, and the shrubs holding still the greenery of Winter, which they never shed. The lily ponds are lying there mucky and black and I wonder when the lilies will be planted. Not before the danger of frost is past, certainly not before the end of May. It will be almost Summer. And I wonder if I will see the gardeners, in their hip boots, walking in the muck, placing lily bulbs in their boxes.

And I think as I stroll amid the lily ponds, around the flower beds, remembering their beauty from the past year, "That which is lost may be recovered." And I pass the canna beds and see that they are already springing through the soil a good inch or two, and it is a sight of both wonder and relief.

I look up and see Shakespeare staring out at me, from his pedestal, and he seems to have weathered the Winter well, and looks smiling on me, knowing that I, too, have weathered the Winter well. Then I see that someone has unkindly written on the base of the pedestal, "Budweiser," where the plaque of Falstaff sets. I walk under a grove of pines, near one of the largest of the gazeboes, the red and white striped one with the ornament top, and smell the scent of pines which tells me it is warm, warmer than the cold spring wind would let you know. It is warm in the ground and in the air, and the pine trees know, and let me smell it.

A flock of pigeons rises up before me and I am in their midst and feel that I am going up with them, am a part of their flock, and they are taking me on their rounds of the park from grove to grove. As they move and dwindle in the distance, I know again that I am earth bound and appropriately attached by a five foot chain to a four-footed animal which, like me, is not only earth bound, but earth bred. So there really cannot be such movement in me as that in the pigeons, much as my curious mind would try. Or could there?

As I watch Herb sniffing close to the ground, I think, "Ah ha! It will not be long before the mushrooms will make their appearance, and I must keep a sharp eye for them among the dead leaves."

I suppose, for me, the wonder of the park is to see each day again what I have seen but did not see. There is a thought I think when I see anew each time, which is that it appears to me that in my other environments I cannot see anew because they are not my environments, but this one, which I choose for myself, can act almost like a magic mirror, and there I can see things new each day that I have seen before but now see again for the first time.

We come to a huge old oak that has leafy buds of red and green, growing in profusion, and nearby the sycamore has not yet come so far, but the swelling at the tips of the twigs reveals that it, too, need not wait too long. And one beyond, a giant white sycamore, against the blue sky and black trees, has four branches stretching into the sky with twigs almost straight up, a magnificent sight. And then I glance to the south and notice for the first time, in this context, two giant smokestacks, as if they were two giant towers guarding the grove that Henry Shaw had set aside. And I glance over at the entrance, and wonder if Henry

8

would have approved of the smokestacks. It's a morning that the air and the feel of it is such that it would not surprise you if some deer should appear, although there are no deer, no animals other than the moles and the squirrels, and others such as the dogs and the cats that occasionally inhabit the park. I think if Henry Shaw were alive that there would be deer in the park, and probably a fence around it to protect it from civilization.

On another day in late February, a Sunday, I went with Herb to the east end of the park and found myself coming up to the Chinese gazebo, which gleams red and gold and green in the sun, looking again at its intriguing surfaces, which tend to bring me back to it time and time again. We can meditate on it a little bit this morning and come back to it later again.

There are some kite-fliers trying to get their kites off the ground. As we come back, there is a young man standing in the Chinese gazebo with a dog on a leash. Two young girls just came down the path. A man in a brown, plastic jacket is sitting on a bench on the Main Drive. Activity is picking up in the park.

Green grass is coming up all over the place, but there are many patches of brown yet. The trees are leafing out a little, budding, the little red buds giving their characteristic color of the early spring. One thing that I notice about the Chinese gazebo is the sheet metal dragons on the ends are all turned inward toward the roof rather than outside, their curved necks pointing toward the center. Nearby, are some beautiful ginkgo trees. We will go over there and see what they are looking like. Their tender tips are just emerging off the short two-inch branches, looking like they might burst at any moment. A robin just swooped out of the tree, flying low, and here is someone nearby sitting with his dog. A tree is lying there with no hint as to where it came from. Going over to the traffic island, which is a nice little oval park to itself, the smell of pines brings back a memory of some pleasant day, which I can't place, but the great pine smell fills the air and returns my day to me.

At the east end of the park, the high gazebo columns sculpture themselves against the snow which fell last night. It is a beautiful example of Moorish style arches and designs. Of course, the pines stand out remarkably and give a vibrance to the whole scene, enhanced by the starkness and severity of the bare deciduous trees.

We are walking now across the snow, which is hard and crunchy. It was soft and wet when it fell, but the overnight freeze has given it this resilient quality, and we see the tracks of men and small animals here and there in the whiteness. And as you walk through the trees they are coming towards you. It requires a small suspense of reason, being on the whiteness, and the trees coming by, to be floating through this white field, or witness trees marching by you, black, one-sided faces, patient, understanding, and a little troubled, perhaps, because of the lateness of the thaw. This blackness of the columnar trees against the whiteness of the field is a mystic majesty that only you can know if you walk through here alone on a snow covered morning. It is at once beautiful, mystifying and inspiring.

You can talk to these trees, whatever period of life you are in, young, middle-aged, or old, and ask them some of their secrets, and perhaps they will speak to you, as they have sometimes to me, but mostly they will reflect to you the silence of your inner being, which is yours alone and so precious to you. And that is another reason it is good to get up in the morning and meet the black columns of trees against the snow, encounter them and speak to them, and see what they have to say to you, or what you have to say to yourself.

I come now to a row of cypress trees, and there is one skinny one here, very thin and sickly looking, almost as if it might have suffered some calamity. It is almost as tall as the tree next to it, but very thin, very wiry, kind of a humped-back tree. There is a ridge that moves out like a spinal column from one side. And I look at it and speak to it, and it talks to me of deprivation, of problems, of patience, and reward perhaps here, not tomorrow, but here.

And, then, close by are the lofty sycamores, with branches that are munificent, that are outreaching, that are embracing, and they speak of openness in man, the willing-ness to accept, and the greatness of being. But at the same time they speak of the resistance of man, of the prejudice they have experienced because of the profusion of their leaves and of their fuzzy seeds. In order to avoid "the mess" these make on city streets where they are planted, many of this generation have rejected them and have had them cut down.

Close by again, in this forest, is a clump of white-bark birches, that are, of course, white, and inoffensive, with small leaves, and that will probably be more accept-able. Suddenly, a different tree rises before me, a tree I do not know, loose, shaggy, disheveled, whose branches, strong main branches and trunk, and very fine smaller branches, look something like a skidrow bum. And I look at it and say, "What are you doing here?" And it does not speak to me. It is just here. It is just being. And it is beautiful. And from the misshapen, rugged, individualist bark, spring the finely etched little branches in many, many divisions, that trace their own artistry and beauty against the sky. And if it does not speak to me, then I say to myself, "Such rugged-ness and individualism can produce beauty."

Herb is patient this morning, as if he knows my whim, not pulling too hard this way or that, stopping with me as I talk to the trees. Now suddenly we are faced with the overpowering presence of a whole phalanx of pin oaks, majestic soldiers whose presence is imposing, and which may make you feel a bit inferior. And if you have problems with authority, you might feel uncomfortable in their pres-ence. However, walk through, enjoy their majesty, and their protection.

Before me now is a grove of pine trees, brilliant green against the snow, and Herb and I walk toward them for refreshment. I find myself under the protective boughs of one tree, behind me the towering pin oaks, and I feel myself embraced by their warm, green needles, the warm green branches, which surround me now, and offer protection. But I know that I cannot remain here, that I must leave, that I must go on, and meet the other trees. I walk out from under the branches, and see another pine tree with a hump back near the base, that speaks perhaps of childhood deformity, disease, or accident. But as I look above it I see that the branches are very green and very full, and that it casts a tremendous protective umbrella far around it. And I marvel at its stamina.

Moving beyond the green canopy I see two strange looking trees at the top of a little slope. At once they speak of novelty and impudence. They have thick trunks until about ten feet above the ground and then branch into two smaller but still thick trunks which twist and turn, but straight towards the heavens, and they look gay and impudent, and individualistic. And they say to me, "We are our own." And I think, this would be a great sight to see before going to work in the morning, to see these trees which are their own masters. And going closer I notice the bark which is close knit, light colored, and has a number of areas which are smooth, as if they had been struck by some calamity that has changed their surface, and I marvel at them and bid good morning to the proud, old catalpa trees.

Going on from there, I see the little stone monuments with snow caps on them, near the eastern gate on Arsenal Street. I walk down the path toward the bridge, and there are thoughts that cannot be spoken, except to trees.

It is early March now, and I return to the park looking for signs of Spring. In a grove of pin oaks it occurs to me that they are so tall and straight that you don't see them too well, and they don't speak to you as much, perhaps, as some of the other trees, which are branching close to the ground. I notice this in a pine tree standing among all of them, very large and very visible.

There goes a lady in a running suit, and a great big dog, kind of dark spotted, like a great dane, walking through the park, two of the inhabitants, looking for Spring.

There are two big trees that have been cut down; you can see the stumps here. They look like they were perfectly healthy, no sign of rotten wood at the base, like diseased elm trees. Another stump over there. It is really sad to see those huge tree stumps, like tombstones, with rugged broken crests where the saws did not quite cut through.

It is the middle of March now, and we had a snow of about five inches last night. Some of it still remains on the ground, patches here and there, and the green is shining out boldly between the patches of white snow. I notice that the cottonwood tree has large buds on it, still tight, not open. The buds on the ginkgo trees are opening. The Chinese gazebo looks festive this morning, with its red roof and gold ribs, with gobs of white snow like whipped cream on the edges, like some kind of a big festive red cake. The red bud trees are coming out here. Small, but fragile dark purple flowers through the black lattice work of the branches of the bare trees around it make an intriguing design and forms a transitory delight in this early spring period.

What have we here? It is a giant oak, at least a hundred years old, that has a limb ripped from its trunk. The limb is gone, but the main trunk goes up about twenty feet of its huge circumference then branches out into two large trunks, and one of them, about twelve feet up, has this gaping hole, about five feet long and two feet wide. From the ground, you can see inside to a depth of about maybe twelve to eighteen inches. You can see how it evidently rotted on the upper portion, at the very top, and then the part that was ripped out, is about four feet long, a tremendous wound in this old living plant. A saddening sight. But, I suppose that the caretakers will repair it, for it certainly is a magnificent tree and deserves all the care it can get.

I am walking across the playing field now. This is, of course, a part of the long, long field that runs all the way from Grand Avenue to Kingshighway. This particular area looks like it is used for soccer. I was just looking around to see if there might be any mushrooms up yet. If the weather had continued warm as it was a few weeks ago, I suppose we would see them, but there are still patches of snow on the ground. I think it is a little too cool for the mushrooms to be bursting forth yet. But they will be soon. You get a checkerboard pattern the way the snow has melted into patches of green and patches of white, a very pretty sight, and one which you can't really enjoy unless you're close to it and walking through it. If you see it snowing, head for Tower Grove Park.

It is now the twenty-first of March, the first day of Spring, and I have just now found a flyer for Six Flags Amusement Park, announcing the world's largest roller coaster, which is certainly a harbinger of Spring. But I have seen other signs of Spring in the park, such as the grass which is high enough to be cut soon. The dandelion flowers have been out for about a week, and already the pods are ready to be blown away in the wind and the seeds scattered all over the park as well as to your lawn and mine. Then there is this weed-like plant which has very purplish flowers, over large areas and forms large patches of purple among the green. And, little things coming up here and there that weren't here last week, or the week before. For instance, as

14

I pause and look down at my feet, I see tiny purple violets peeping up through the grass, and they are scattered about here and there, to give a little dash of color and accent to the park floor. Here and there redbud trees, all in bloom, beautiful against the dark green pines. The trees are putting forth quite a drapery of green, that whispy green of early Spring you know, among the branches, which kind of tantalizes you into the feeling of Spring from the Winter doldrums, deep inside your body.

It is such a great morning that I make up a little song and sing it to myself. It doesn't happen every day, and I don't really think about it, but it is a wonderful thing to be able to walk in the park and make up songs and sing them to yourself. It's something that just happens.

A few days after the official opening of Spring, I am approaching the park from the Roger Place entrance. There is a great deal of cleaning up going on, right at the entrance, like a spring cleaning. There is a fellow cleaning out leaves from around the trees, a couple of attendants, a truck, some kind of a machine that goes over the ground, putting little holes in it, aerating the soil. They are doing a fine job of cleaning up the park and I have never seen that kind of an operation before.

Well, it is Early Spring, and the leaves are coming out on the maples, very heavy now, the mulberry, the Osage orange, both have a lot of green coming out of them. I move over toward the big "King Oak" to see how it looks after the Winter. I am at a ginkgo tree which has very heavy overhanging branches, and I can see the buds up close. They are very full, ready to pop out. I can see the green coming out of the various trees. I would like to be able to come back and watch it day by day, in the same place.

There's the "King Oak." It seems to have weathered the Winter pretty well. No limbs missing or out of place. One is hanging down, but it is the same one that has been dangling there for some time. The tree is beautiful in its articulation against the sky. It is something that must be seen at this time of year, or in the Winter, as well as in the Summer, to appreciate fully its majestic beauty.

The "King Oak"

A small bird just flew in at high tree top level. I can't make it out completely, but it has a yellow breast. Robins are on the ground everywhere. Herb is digging moles everywhere. Spring is sprung, the birds are come. The park is just a scene of idyllic beauty at this time of year.

That looks like a mushroom, but is just a seed pit. I haven't seen any mushrooms in this park, as often as I come here, this Spring. Squirrels are running all around, up and down the trees, in a kind of a network. I like this time of the year very much because you can see so many things at the same time; it gives you a feeling of being all together with nature. It is like a different era altogether, like being in the midst of a Victorian city, I can see the statue of von Humboldt, three gazeboes, and the Music Stand, all at the same time, a vista that is not often found in the city.

Early April finds me in the midst of Tower Grove Park on a balmy Spring day, and you might say that this is the day that Spring really arrived in Tower Grove Park. In fact, all of the trees are putting out some leaves. There are leaves on every shrub and the grass is up. In bloom are the tulips, the jonquils, the hyacinths, and it's just beautiful. The youngsters are out playing softball. It's a scene hard to describe, but you have an impression of all the bareness and blackness of Winter, suddenly turning alive and green. It's incredible. And on the green park floor you have the innumerable violets and dandelion flowers, we used to call them buttercups, adding to this tremendous display of beauty. The squirrels are just about everywhere. Herb is shaking all over, and he is full of the Spring season too.

Passing by the "King Oak" I notice that it has a trace of greenery on its stark, bare branches. It's going to be another beautiful year for old "King Oak." The branches on the Osage orange are turning green, no leaves, but the wood of the branches is taking on a greenish hue. There, in the distance, I can see a tree with big pods on it, which might be a honey locust tree.

At the Music Stand we have a circle of tulip magnolias, blooming profusely. Here's a ginkgo coming out. It's interesting to see how the leaves come out of those little tips, something that looks like little tassels, about six on a pod, a very pretty sight, and an interesting sight just at this time of year. There are little tail-like things coming out of the center. That's the first time I have ever seen it. But that is the wonder of the park. There is always something new!

Now, right by the Chinese gazebo, I am in the midst of a flock of birds with yellow breasts and pointed beaks. They won't stand still long enough to see what kind they are. Those over there are young starlings. There are three of them in the maple tree next to the Chinese gazebo.

Across the Walking Road from the Chinese gazebo looms a structure which is new and appears rather strange. Tall posts support a bar and chains with rings hanging down from it. Is it some instrument of torture devised by unseen inhabitants of the nearby gazebo? Not to fear. It is only one of a series of similar type structures called a "Parcourse," designed for those who wish to strengthen their bodies in extraordinary ways. I have, on occasion, tried one or two of the devices, and, for me, they are torture. Although some of my walking companions seem to enjoy them, I will stick to walking. I muse that some far-off day, some yet-to-be-born archeologist will puzzle over the concrete foundations and declare that they were once used for "ritual purposes."

We are coming on to a field where I have not walked before, right across from a street whose name I am going to find, after you pass a clump of trees on Arsenal Street. It's Portis Avenue. And there again is one of the long fields after a nicely spaced grove of trees, so characteristic of the landscaping in the park. It's been raining all night, and the water is standing here, there and everywhere. They are doing a lot of work replacing curbs, putting stone curbs in, similar to the originals. This is an historic landmark and they are preserving it as it has been, and it is marvelous.

On a Friday in March, in the southwest part of the park, a place where I am very seldom found, across the road from the rest rooms, I found the "grave marker" that people have asked me about. It says "Elizah Hoope 1882" and that's all that's on it. There is a sunken area, about six feet long, by the marker, and I have not noticed that as long as I have been here. The park superintendent informs me that the ''grave marker'' is actually a marker for a tree planting, the tree evidently not surviving. So I guess we could call it a grave marker for a tree.

Over here is Picnic Area X on the edge of a little stream, which used to flow through the park, and still does when it rains. A clump of birch along the creek, all still bare, are very pretty, white, svelte, smooth-barked trees. To me they are very feminine. And close-by, a gnarled little tree, looks like a willow, has a branch like a corkscrew, a heavy one. Just a little bit west there's a rivulet that runs into the creek. The stream here is like a brook with clear water running through it. It looks beautiful. You can almost believe you are in a rural setting, another pleasure of this park designed for the relief of ''work-weary folk.''

# The Park
# In Late Spring

*"Plants are God's text-books wherein He has written life's secrets. If you would know how to live, study the trees and flowers."—James Gurney*

It is a late May Sunday morning in Tower Grove Park, and Sunday takes on a special meaning. The park has a different atmosphere, a different presence about it. We are at the east end of the park near Arsenal Street. It has been a beautiful May, very warm, with some cool breezes, and this morning is one of those mornings, about ten o'clock, bright sunlight with light breezes cooling things.

Late Spring is wonderful in St. Louis and especially in Tower Grove Park. In my childhood, Sunday in the park meant Sherman Park in north St. Louis where my Dad would often take us, sometimes in the morning to play Indian ball, sometimes in the afternoon to watch the professional ball games of the City League. And I remember the grandstands full of people, and the ice cream carts. Occasionally, we would get an ice cream if we could afford a nickel in those Depression days. Sunday was a very special day.

Here in Tower Grove Park all of the leaves are out, of course, new and shiny, no hot blast of wind against them yet, no dust of drought blurring or dulling their surfaces. They are shining and pristine as they should be in late Spring. We come by a grove of trees which look particularly graceful this morning, their trunk bodies leaning this way and that, spaced fairly wide apart, standing like motionless ballet dancers or wood nymphs in the landscape.

Close by Grand Avenue and Arsenal Street there is a small children's playground right off the path. The large gazebo is up ahead, and it has been remodeled so we will go and see what they have done to it. The roofs have been completed and the shelter repainted in shades of brown. I just saw a small white magnolia blossom in a clump of tree trunks. The statue of Christopher Columbus looms up before us, its granite base gleaming pinkish in the sun. A motorcycle is parked nearby with two sparkling helmets dangling from the back, a sure sign of late Spring. The Messiah Lutheran Church across Grand Avenue is having services, drawing parked cars around the park entrance. One man is polishing his car, another sign of late Spring.

It feels almost like Summer is here. There are several people sunbathing in the park today. The grass is taking on the deep humid smell of Summer. It has been cut and gives off the aroma of new mown hay, so different from the musty first smell of Spring when the grass is first coming out.

We just passed by the boat pond area and the fountain which will soon be the scene of frequent visits by wedding parties, taking pictures against the backdrop of the ruins and the pond. The tennis courts and children's playground in the main circle area are filled with people, and the drives are filled with cars and people are carrying things from them into the main picnic area.

It is a Monday now in late Spring. A whole troop of squirrels is running around between two trees, amid the picnic litter from Sunday. A few weeks ago the poplar trees were in bloom with their waxy white tulip-like flowers with yellow centers in profusion. Also one tree near the east entrance to the park, with pink blossoms covering it, a horse chestnut, made a striking appearance.

Another sign of late Spring is the digging up of the lily ponds, the workers making trenches and little mounds of soil in preparation of planting the water lilies. There is water coming out of a pipe, in one pond, starting to fill it up. The water runs from there into the other ponds. There are no lilies in the pots as yet, which have been prepared for planting. Water is in the bullrushes here, where someone has made a path.

Walking east to the middle of the park we find a big piece of tree stump lying in the non-vehicular road. Herb sniffs it quizzically, and evidently wonders, as I do, how it got there. It was probably on the grass and some arboreal enthusiasts pulled it over into the road, a big job, because it is heavy. In the wooded area, just east of the Chinese gazebo, three crows are flying about and calling loudly. Something must have happened, perhaps a fledgling out of the nest, although I could not see one on the ground. Yesterday I saw one, too young to fly, on the ground, in another part of the park.

Now we are under a large tree with heart-shaped leaves, and it has little blossoms on it which are just delicious smelling. It is a linden tree, like the ones described in the bower of three trees on the First Walk. It usually flowers in June, but the exceptionally warm May has brought out the blooms already, two weeks early. The flowers provide an excellent honey, and the bees are already busy on this one.

Walking along the field that stretches on the Arsenal Street side from Oak Hill to Bent, I found a tree with seven trunks which I thought worth noting. I saved a leaf, looked it up, and it appears that it might be a service-berry. A little farther west we find an old gnarled tree trunk with living green branches remarkably coming forth from it, and huge clusters of white blossoms speckled with yellow and violet. It is a catalpa, and next to it another tree of the same kind is in full bloom. Up close, the blossoms look like tiny orchids. Hearing the sound of water, I glance toward the boat pond and see that the fountain has been turned on. Summer is coming fast.

On the last Saturday morning in May I go through the Roger Place entrance, through the low bushes by a mulberry tree, and am overpowered by a sweet smell. I can't make out where it is coming from for I can't see any blossoms. It may just be from the mulberries, although I don't remember their ever giving off such fragrance. Looking at the Osage orange trees, I notice that the leaves are not very full. I want to look closely at those leaves, and see what they are like. The leaves are not like the mulberry, even though it is from the mulberry family. The leaves are oblong and pointed, whereas the mulberries are heart shaped.

It is a beautiful late Spring morning in May and I am walking basically the route of the First Walk, in at Roger Place and cutting over west by north, to the big bushy oak, and this brings me into view now of the Giant "King Oak" which is in all its foliage splendor. The air is moist and warm, but there is a slight breeze which tends to make it bearable. I hadn't really noticed it before but there is a cluster of birch-like trees around the "King Oak" just to the east of it, semicircular, very nice, with green berries on them, and narrow, heart-shaped leaves coming to an extreme point, with saw-toothed edges. The bark is mottled and grayish. They must be hackberry trees.

I am now in a grove of poplars in the traffic circle, and these poplars are also known as tulip trees. Here in late May I am looking at a tulip tree, and it has already bloomed and the flowers are gone, and now there is a little bullet-shaped pod where the flowers were, and perhaps that will be the seed. There are a few flowers on a branch of this tree, and a green cone grows in the center of the flower and evidently emerges and grows after the petals fall off. Some of the old dried flowers are still on the tree with small pointed needle-like seeds inside them.

Here is a low, about fifteen feet tall, magnolia with waxy white, small flowers. It may be the Sweetbay variety. In the canna lily bed, by the Music Stand, there is one canna lily blooming, very pretty. The cactus type plant is blooming. It looks like a Spanish bayonet, but it has a long stem and big white flowers on it.

The lily ponds are partially planted, with markers sticking up out of the water indicating the planters yet to be placed. Just a few leaves are floating on the water where the plants have been put in. In the canna beds only one bright red flower is standing up. In the lily pond closest to the main traffic circle, there is gravel on the bottom, rather than the muck on the bottom of the other ponds.

Over in the main traffic circle the giant elm tree is standing fast, with the base for a plaque which was stolen still beneath it. The mulberry tree, with the marker, is over 100 years old. It is full of mulberries, and I notice that the leaves of this mulberry tree are different than those I am used to seeing in southern Illinois. These are broad-shaped leaves, about four inches in length. Lots of mulberries. I'll try some. They are juicy and sweet and really taste good. Should have some of these for breakfast. I better quit. They are really sweet. There is a copper beech, which I had not noticed before. It has the characteristic reddish brown leaves, and many branches from the trunk, starting close to the ground. The flag is still flying rather listlessly from the tall pole; it stirs once in awhile. There are also several reddish leaved maples here. Leaving the traffic circle we are now by a very beautiful tree east of the largest picnic shelter. It has many small branches, low, very thick, an oak. Herb has been digging here under these linden trees, near the Walking Road. He is tired now and is lying down to rest at the edge of the linden tree and the field, and I am sitting here at a little opening in the bower, a little window on the field, under the protection of the tree.

It is the last Sunday in May. It is difficult to describe the beauty of the park on a Sunday morning, especially an early Sunday morning. It is not eight o'clock yet, and I am in the long field on the Arsenal Street side, between Roger Place and Bent Avenue. The sun is high already and burning off a slight haze. There is no one here except Herb and myself. Again, the colors, I can only compare to a romantic landscape painting, Rousseau or Constable or even Reubens.

There is nothing like a romantic landscape on an early Spring Sunday morning to put one in a reminiscing mood. I was reading some old letters last night, very old, written during World War II, and they come back now to me in this peaceful setting. I had just been sent to Navy boot camp, and the letters were from a very good friend and confidant who was age eighteen, and I was age nineteen. All the letters I had, of course, were from my friend, and it was interesting, from the things that he wrote to try to reconstruct the way that I felt and some of the things that were important to us then. Some of them now seem trivial, and others simply seem to have been obliterated, run over in the race of life, for life. And I guess that is one of the reasons I keep returning to the park, daily, now twice daily, perhaps to find that piece of me, or any pieces of me that I would still like to remember, from a time when things seemed much more intense, much more important, and alive, and coming over here can't recapture that, but somehow, it brings me to that, to that period of my life, and the environment helps me remember. That was thirty-four years ago, a long time. I guess the memory cells are there, all information encoded, available, if you can retrieve it.

I just remember, from that time, seeing particular things, not too much of anything really. But I remember playing the Peer Gynt Suite on the old seventy-eight rpm gramophone at this lady's house we used to go to in Aviston, Illinois. She was a friend of the family's who used to take care of us children at times. And then after I went into the service, my young correspondent continued to go there, taking my parents, who could not drive. And then, a few months later, we were both in the service, and a little after that the lady died. I was gone for three years in the Navy after that, and how sad it seems now, that I did not have time for thinking of her until today. There are so many pieces of our lives that seem unfinished.

Here at the boat pond the water is clear and clean. It's been cleaned up considerably since I looked at it last week. There are a number of people at the pond; people sitting and walking, and the goldfish, of course, are swimming. There's someone sleeping on the hummock at the lily ponds. A tree in the center of the hummock has golden spikelets of flowers all over it. The canna lily that was here yesterday is gone; petals fallen to the ground mark its remembrance.

It is a great Memorial Day morning here in Tower Grove Park. We approach the Music Stand and the boat pond, from the statue of von Humboldt. It is delightfully cool, the sun just getting up above the trees, and a very light breeze on your skin. The canna lily bed by the Music Stand has three bright red flowers in the center and there is a fourth one coming up just off the center there, looking very regal and ready for the start of a whole new day.

On the little hummock by the lily ponds and the boat pond there is an interesting tree with notched, ragged heart-shaped leaves. It has small, about a half inch across, fruits which look like rose hips. It appears to be a species of hawthorne. The golden flowering tree is there as we saw yesterday. (Later, I went to Shaw's Garden and learned that it is a Golden Rain tree.) Nearby is a mulberry with giant fruits on it, beautiful, about three quarters of an inch long, nice, round, and plump. Among the ground cover I see a few little yellow flowers in a plant that has three leaves, each divided into two, making it heart-shaped. It's really pretty. I need to look at the ground more; there are lots of things going on in the ground.

Just east of the Oak Hill entrance there is a grove of oak trees and one of them, quite large, is dead. Completely dead. May be diseased. What happened to it? Trying to see some sign of life. It is very dead. I didn't know an oak tree could die like that. The elms are looking very bad this time of year. I think the worms have been at them. They all look terrible. The little white bell-shaped flowers are out this morning. Very pretty on the ground.

It's a Sunday afternoon and we are at the Main Drive traffic circle in front of the Shakespeare statue. Through traffic has been stopped and there are about 200 people here, standing, a few with bicycles and some with chairs for the Shakespeare Festival. The players are being introduced and the various scenes from Shakespeare's plays to be performed on the Music Stand are announced. There are many older and younger people here, people with baby carriages, with dogs, with bicycles, with lawn chairs, and transistor radios. It's a warm but mild day with a bit of a breeze. Some men are dressed in suits, but it is comfortable with a light shirt or a light coat of some kind.

Now, at the Music Stand, the players are assembled. About 300 persons are gathered around, most of them standing attentive, trying to hear the dramatic performances with some difficulty because of the noise in the crowd, people talking to one another. Plus, the people walking around the gravel path make a shuffling sound on the gravel. I remember Irma Tucker, director of City Players of St. Louis, telling about putting on a play in the park and the trouble they had with noise and scenery blowing down.

Most of the people are here, apparently, specifically for the performance. Occasionally someone wanders in from the perimeter and asks what is going on. People inform them that it is the rededication of the Shakespeare statue. There are people with cameras, taking pictures, in addition to the TV cameras covering the event. With the last presentation, "Catherine of Aragon," a number of the people are leaving, but still a substantial group continues to watch.

The park is the site of so many ceremonies and customs, some of which I have seen, like the Shakespeare Festival, neighborhood fairs, and Columbus Day activities around the statue of Columbus. Once there was an international fair at which I saw a polo match for the first time. If the trees could tell us they would have much to say about the activities in Tower Grove Park over the years. There was square dancing in the park, regular classes on Mondays and Fridays, when that was popular in the 1940's, under the direction of Mrs. Helen Dunbar. In the Palm House, across the road north of the lily ponds, dramatizations of books were performed. Walter ("Doc") Eberhardt of St. Louis University was giving physical fitness classes in the park about that time also. Sunrise services were conducted on Easter morning with thousands in attendance. Shakespeare was honored regularly by the drama class of Webster College when the girls placed a wreath at the statue of Shakespeare every year. Book reviews, group singing, and children's amateur hours were all part of the entertainment of the day, before television.

The "Neighborhood News" in its 1947, twenty-fifth anniversary edition declared "Tower Grove Park is a family park . . . It possesses all the homey charm of a comfortable back yard." One of the most remarkable activities it reported was what it called "wood chopping picnics" after the storm of September 1, 1946 on a Sunday afternoon. Freak winds uprooted or snapped off 160 trees in the park that day. People came with basket lunches, axes and saws to clean up the destruction and hauled away all the debris they could. Those were different times with different needs and different ways of meeting them.

Across the drive from the boat pond area, walking east and south, it's a cool morning in June. Approaching one of the picnic gazeboes in late Spring on a cool morning with the fresh green smells of the trees and the grass, new mown grass around you, is a singular experience. You have the shadows and sunlight casting interesting patterns. Across the way the squirrels are standing motionless and the birds are sitting all around. There is no one here at all, to wait in expectation of a lovely late Spring day.

The beauty of this morning is difficult to describe. If you can think of cool air, and a breeze whispering through the trees, the sunlight almost like liquid, striping the green tree floors, and shadows that are thick with cloying smells, you might describe, minutely, the scene before me on a late Spring morning. It's a morning like you could walk forever, and you just want to walk, and walk, and walk. It's great. Herb is going to walk forever, somewhere else, after a mole. There's another gnarled old catalpa tree, near a gazebo on the north side not far east of the Music Stand. The catalpas seem so beaten up.

On the first Sunday morning in June, at the east end of Tower Grove Park, it's a warm, humid Sunday morning. Standing here under a very large catalpa tree, the blossoms are gone, but here is a wrinkled looking, fingerlike appendage coming out at the end of the stems. It will be interesting to see how that develops during the next few weeks. Walking now under the druid circle of trees, I realize that it's the first time I've walked under the arching branches, which bend to the outside of the semi-circle. It's very inviting, a little tunnel of green. Herb started digging here and that is how I happen to be here. Evidently, there are some ceremonials conducted here, because there are little pieces of broken glass scattered all over the ground, although there are no rocks here on which to break bottles. They probably have been broken on the trees. Someone is preparing a picnic here, at the pavilion, with crepe paper decorations, yellow and green, some young people and some a little older, perhaps a family celebration. They appear to be getting ready for a larger group.

The carillon of the Lutheran Church peals now, and you can hear it if you listen a minute. Standing here under a big poplar tree, there are about half a dozen crows carrying on, three of them sitting in a row. They heard me talking and then took off and started flying around. It's really weird, seeing these big birds sitting above your head. Suspiciously, I wonder if they will attack, as in the movie, "The Birds."

We come to the end of late Spring on a Monday morning in Tower Grove Park. Coming in at the Roger Place entrance, I move to the traffic island where the statue of von Humboldt stands. Over at the north end, about one hundred feet from the statue, is a very large maple that is broken off about twenty feet from the base. It looks like it was rotted out, or had a piece torn out of it some time ago. It started to heal over, but it was too weak. The wind must have gotten it. As we move toward Summer, I think that this season, too, can be beautiful, but unkind.

*The Music Stand*

# The Park In Summer

*"For every phase in the human life, there is a parallel in plant life."*—James Gurney

Although it is not the twenty-first of June, school is out, so it must be Summer. There is an Antique Auto Show and Flea Market here in Tower Grove Park today. This seems to herald the beginning of the Summer season in the park, which will have mostly to do with people and events, rather than trees and plants. The Walking Road has been opened especially for this occasion, and cars are parked all the way from Center Cross Drive to the first traffic island and a little beyond, to the big "King Oak."

The theme of this exposition is antique autos, mostly old Fords. Much of the flea market offerings consist of old automobile parts. There are old chassis on flat bed trailers, which are not for sale, pieces of cars, doors, fenders, hub caps, and engine parts. It really looks junky and I wondered if, with our love of things, rather than nature, if the park might someday become a junk yard?

It is now Tuesday in the middle of June and we are in the first traffic circle, on the north side, walking north into the field by the North Drive. Over here is a huge mulberry tree, that has a split in the middle and big chunks out of it, but still thriving, with branches reaching all the way down to the ground. The thing that I notice about it is that the mulberries are not yet ripe, and all the other mulberry trees I have seen were ripe long ago. These are still green and there are no red berries on it. I think, perhaps, it is a white mulberry tree.

Over here on the north side there is a nice open field, stretching from Magnolia Avenue, which is lined with trees to a depth of about twenty-five feet in the park, to the North Drive. It is a very pleasant field, not as intriguing in landscaping as those on the south side, and with not nearly the amount of wide open space, but a nice small field, heavily bordered with trees which screen it from the street.

I am looking now at some of the big houses on Magnolia Avenue, noting the stained glass work on the portals of some of the windows, some very lovely blues, and one has a brick arch porch in front, and another arch over the lower window, and small colonnades on the second story porch, which are quite unusual. This particular house is directly east of the Tower Grove Baptist Church, a large multi-building complex that stretches for several hundred yards on the north side of Magnolia Avenue.

Walking west on Magnolia Avenue on the park side, by a chain-link fence, I find myself by the house that was built according to Henry Shaw's plan of developing English manor houses on leased land around the park. Shaw's plan was based on the English method of leasing land on the perimeter of a park, with the hope that people would pay for the privilege of building there. However, it did not work out in Tower Grove Park. This was the only house that was built, and Henry Shaw built it as a model house. It has housed the superintendents of Tower Grove Park for the last hundred odd years. The yard has an iron fence around it, ivy on the ground and a beautiful golden rain tree in the front yard. On the west corner there is a high iron fence with spikes, which is a part of the park fence also. Then the seclusion of the house is continued by a chain-link fence along the park side.

Shaw reserved a 200 foot perimeter around the park for the purpose of building "villas" on the leased land, but he also offered to rescind this requirement if the city would build an iron fence around the park. The city did not and later purchased the 200 foot strip from the Missouri Botanical Garden, the designated beneficiary if the land were not leased.

Near the corner of North Drive and Center Cross Drive is a large golden rain tree which is fully in bloom, a truly magnificent sight. On a June day, when you get over to the park, you might want to look for it. And here is a tree next to the boat pond, that looks like a buckeye with its five pointed leaflets reaching out like a human hand. It has a hard fruit with a prickly brown surface with a white spot, from which it gets its name.

In the center of the park on the north side, it is another nice cool day, a Wednesday, here in St. Louis. The temperature is in the sixties to low seventies. It really feels fine. A morning like this makes you appreciate the poets when they render such a phrase as "Shall I compare you to a Summer's day?" because a Summer's day like this is ineffable, and cannot be spoken or described. Comparing someone to a Summer's day, like this, is indeed a high compliment, an extreme compliment.

The trees being full with leaves now gives us a chance to see their silhouettes in their full foliage. We come to a ginkgo tree which is quite old and has many branches, thick trunks coming out at the base. It has a fine pyramidal shape, almost the shape of a Christmas tree, a beautiful tree, right near the gazebo on the north side just east of the boat pond. Here is another one of those trees with the heart-shaped leaves and narrow pale green seed pods. They must be linden trees. I saw two big ones yesterday and here are two smaller ones. One of the nice things about being here in Tower Grove Park is that Shaw's Garden is close by and very often I can go over there and check out the trees, because they have all kinds of trees over there with names tacked right on them.

I am walking along the path from that gazebo, near the North Drive, leading up to the Music Stand, and here is a tree with multiple leaves, and many yellow-red berries. The bark looks somewhat like a cherry. It may be a

European mountain ash. And over here, not far from the gazebo, back east a bit, is a buckeye tree. And here is a tree which must be a wild cherry, judging from the bark, although it does not have any fruit on it. It has a big split down the side and a lot of sap oozing out. There is a double row of these trees, lining both sides of the path as we approach the Music Stand from the east.

Nearby is a catalpa tree which doesn't have any seed pods on it, but about fifteen feet away are four catalpas and they have the long seed pods on them, or "lady cigars" as we called them as kids, and I suppose those were the finger like growths we saw just a couple of weeks ago. They are now quite long, and green, and these are the seeds of the catalpa. Its original range was in the southeast United States, and the catalpa family is well known in the tropics. The seed pods are about a foot long, and very pretty.

The high cottonwood tree just north of the Music Stand has leafed out. It is very wide in diameter, and has some interesting trunk-like branches about twenty feet above the ground. It is one of the largest cottonwoods, a species not often represented, in the park.

Back here near the main entrance area there is a tree stump and some little blue flowers, with just two petals opposite one another, quite charming, on a stalk that looks like a long grass stem with wide blades on it.

This seems to be a morning that I feel like singing, and I have been singing ever since I got up, which I haven't done for quite a while. I enjoy that. Over by the Music Stand they keep the grass cut and they must water the grass around here, as I have seen sprinklers out around the ponds.

Moving away from the Music Stand, north over toward Magnolia Avenue, there is another small field, which is really larger than it appears. There is a little clearing here because it is kind of pinched in by trees, but then it opens up into a magnificent field, which continues for about a block. I move back over to the Music Stand, noticing that there are few people here. I glance at my watch and see that it is only eight a.m.

It is Wednesday, the day after Summer officially begins. In Tower Grove Park there is a beautiful cloudy morning sky after a heavy rain last night; the first good rain we have had in maybe six weeks or longer. We are in the middle of the park, on the south side, in a grove of pin oaks. The park after a rain is very pretty as the trees, with their wetted surfaces look very black and are in great contrast to the wetness of the green grass. It smells good too.

I have gone east now and am over by the sacred grove or druid circle of trees, as I call it, and am looking at the Osage orange trees, which are striped orange and black as they are wet, the darker part of the bark taking on a very dark color, almost black, while the yellow part is accentuated, so they look kind of orangish-yellow and black. One of the trees has some large fruit on it and it is the only one that has. With the ground being so wet once again, it is very good mole hunting for Herb, and I have taken him to some choice mole hunting spots where there are many burrows. And, sure enough, right under the sacred grove, he found one. He doesn't want to let go of it now, but he finally lets go and starts hunting again.

Under the ginkgo tree, here after the heavy rain, is one of the green fruit from this tree, lying on the ground. They are green now, but in the Fall will turn into an evil-smelling yellowish, soft fruit. And over here, having crossed Main Drive to the north side, there is an interesting tree with three trunks, and being wet, it has a reddish-brown look. Its leaves are oval, pointed, with leaflets which are alternately spaced. And next to it is a tree with a similarly colored trunk, but the bark is much rougher, in larger segments and seems to be thicker. The leaves are very similar, but this tree has big seed pods which resemble the Kentucky Coffee tree seeds. And just north of that, a few feet, is what must be the largest tulip poplar tree in the park. I am trying to estimate its circumference now, walking around it, and it must be eighteen or twenty feet in circumference. Someday I am going to come over to the park with a tape measure and measure all of the large trees.

We have crossed over now to the third traffic island from the center of the park, and this island is one I don't get into very often. But it is delightful, right now, in the midst of these giant cypress trees, and their size is unbelievable. Very few people, I think, walk through these islands, at least I don't see very many. To walk among these cypress trees, which are about sixty feet tall and ten or twelve feet in circumference, is like walking into another world, a mini-world and it's something to think about when you come to the park. You can find, and perhaps create, all kinds of little worlds, just by walking a few feet from the beaten path.

Walking down the Walking Road now, going west, where the road bends and curves, on the side towards Arsenal Street, we come to three large linden trees, in a triangle. These old linden trees form a bower, under which there has been a picnic table, which may still be there. It is a favorite trysting place for lovers. In the warm June air the tiny but profuse blossoms of the linden tree give off a perfume that is sweet and memorable. Some years they blossom in late May.

I learned that the linden tree blossoms may be used to make a tea. A couple I met at the Music Stand said that in Europe the flowers are dried and used to make a tea which is good for a sore throat. The couple is from the Ukraine. They have lived near the park for 17 years, raised a family, three children, and they use the park almost every day. They said that the woman's mother has special names for certain areas of the park and that other people they know have their own names for various parts of the park.

It is a Thursday morning in June, by the gazebo on the north side of the traffic island with the von Humboldt statue. Here by an elm tree I find the first mushrooms I have seen in the park this year. They are coprinus or "inky caps." Some are in prime condition, others are wilting away into the inky blob that they eventually become.

We had another rain last night. That's two nights in a row. This one was not quite so heavy as the first one we had, so maybe we will see some new life forms, that is, new to the park this season, especially mushrooms. Some more small mushrooms are on the ground, thin stems, brown caps, white gills, which I can't identify off hand.

There is a giant Osage orange tree on the north side of the park just a little north and west of the Thurmond Street entrance at Magnolia. Going now through a beautiful field, going up from Thurmond to Tower Grove, or rather to a grove of trees across from the Music Stand. Here's a little tree with some fruit, which looks like crab apple.

We are right across from a rather interesting housing development, Hortus Court, which is a walkway with an entrance flanked by two brick towers. And there are very nice, two story Cape Cod type houses, six of them, along the walk, three on each side. They have small front yards, perhaps twenty feet deep, and no back yards. The back has a drive or alley. A very interesting housing concept which I don't recall seeing elsewhere in the city. It would be interesting to know how that was developed. It was probably before the present zoning laws. The drives are only wide enough for a single car. So I assume the drives do not serve any purpose for those houses and the people who live in them must park their cars on Magnolia Avenue.

There are two mansions which look like fraternal twins, on the northeast corner of Klemm and Magnolia. The facades are not exactly the same but certainly bear a striking resemblance with similar brickwork and red granite-like columns.

This is the third night in a row we had rain, and it is still raining now, a Friday morning in late June, just east of the Music Stand, walking under a big buckeye tree, I now pass a couple of trees with some twine tied around them, which look like they might have been used for a net. The sound of thunder, or jet airplanes, fills the air. The park in the rain is just a great dreary, wonderful place to be. A time to be melancholy, but light hearted about it at the same time, like the feeling of melancholy you get when listening to "Gloomy Sunday." I should look for some mushrooms with all this rain. I am surprised there aren't any field mushrooms, but I haven't seen any this year.

It is the morning after the Fourth of July and I have made an interesting discovery here, in the south side of the park just below the administration building, under an oak tree. A very interesting mushroom with yellow caps, conical when just emerging, then splitting as the caps spread out, and opening like the petals of a flower. I haven't seen anything quite like it before. It is a hot, muggy day. The temperature didn't go below eight-two last night and early this morning it got down to seventy-eight. We are now right behind the old "King Oak" tree, approaching from the far side, the north side, and it is still an impressive sight. Oh! it has a face on the north side! I have never noticed that before, because I usually approach from the other side. It has a very sad face, two eyes which are not in line, a very thick brow, and a nose that kind of goes in, and a small frowning mouth! That is remarkable. If you stand on the northwest side, by the small maple, and not far from the path, you can see the face very distinctly right below the branches. In fact, one branch comes out just about the top of the middle of his head. The face of the King of the park is sad.

Seeing that sad tree face, in these beautiful surroundings, I think of the people with illnesses and handicaps who worked to overcome them. Darwin evidently was an invalid. There were others who were obstacles to themselves. And then I thought how sad it is to have a sickness without symptoms, the sickness that robs us of creativity and keeps us from realizing our full potential, the sickness that no doctors know or can cure, and which can only be cured by the individual himself.

What is that sickness? It is a hardening of perception and being no longer able to perceive, to see but not be seeing, to want to feel but not be feeling. There's an illness that is not fatal, but lingering.

On a warm evening in July I walk with another companion, my wife, to Tower Grove Park. We are carrying our folding chairs and joining hundreds of others to hear a Summer concert in the park by the Compton Heights band. All of the parking spaces around the pond are taken. People in light Summer clothes are seated on park benches and folding chairs to listen to the enthralling music, the stirring marches, the sweet melodies, the charming songs, all played by the Compton Heights Band. For several years the band has been playing in the park, and other public places. The conductor, Kaid Friedel, is in the French horn section of the St. Louis Symphony orchestra. He has brought together a fine company of over seventy volunteer musicians with a repertoire of music that is a delight to young and old. Stirring marches are followed by familiar musicals and the program is highlighted by soloists in symphonic renditions. Seated in the circle around the Music Stand, the dim street lights overhead, the crickets chirping, the children frolicking in the grass, the dogs walking inquiringly through the crowd, and everyone attentive, brings one back to the early days when Henry Shaw first dedicated the Music Stand, and the music stirs anew as it did then, and the park is alive once more.

A long awaited event of Summer has arrived in Tower Grove Park, In the middle of July, I am standing by the lily ponds and the first small white lilies are rising above the surface, poking their heads above the water. They are scattered here and there, and, of course, they are planted in pots within the ponds, the water in the ponds circulating. The shape of the ponds is quite pleasing to the eye. One has a long goose neck that comes around and then branches out to two shorter blunt points. Another kidney-shaped pond is nestled close by. One more is far over to the south, and it is a larger kidney-shaped pond with larger bulbous ends. All of these are filled with small white and purple flowers. Later on the reds and yellows will come out, and the flowers will become much larger. It is quite a beautiful sight, and many visitors will be stopping by.

The sight of these water lilies used to be a rather rare thing. I can remember coming here as a child. We would drive all the way from north St. Louis to Tower Grove Park just to see the water lilies. There are still not many places where you can see them, although displays are available in other parts of the city, including Shaw's Garden.

In the main traffic circle there is a tall new flag pole with an ornamental base set on a foundation of flag stones. Proudly, from the top, flies a great flag of the United States, proclaiming the fulfillment of the promise and the dream that Henry Shaw found in this country and so gratefully repaid with the park and the garden. A plaque at the bottom says, "Dedicated 8 August, 1982 in honor of Gerhardt Kramer, devoted Commissioner of Tower Grove Park." Nearby, two trees bearing plaques stand near a venerable maple forming an ancient tree triad. The maple has a gaping wound in its side, which, with its two outstretched arms, gives it a grotesque appearance worthy of a Disney animator.

As we come into the entrance off Roger Place, I see a stout, short little man, in a ball player cap, with a metal detector. As I walk toward the northeast, I hear the clank of iron against iron, the horseshoe players, up where the regular Sunday morning horseshoe games are played. The Summer storms have wreaked their havoc, and we pass by the stump of a once large towering tree, that has been newly cut. Its base is firm and unriddled by rot, or breakage, and I suspect that lightening has played a part in its demise. There are branches down from the storm. This was one of the heaviest downpours of water in a short space of time in many years, the first time that our basement has ever been flooded.

Crossing over at the second traffic circle, going east, I see another tree freshly cut, this one chopped down, about eighteen inches in diameter. The replacement of trees goes on continuously in the park. Many of those trees standing were planted by Henry Shaw himself. In the late Summer season we see beer and soda cans galore, some of them chopped up into bizarre shapes of tin by the mowing machines.

We come now to one of the little gazeboes, the twin to the one on the other side of the traffic circle. Incidentally, all of the paths have been blacktopped and graveled, in the style in which they had originally been designed, and look very bright and attractive. We come to another tree stump, this one quite large, at least twenty-eight or thirty inches in diameter. Beautiful ginkgoes and poplars surround us, weeping willow, giant pin oaks, near the silent stump. A slight breeze, letting warm moisture come up from the Mississippi River, fans my cheeks. The humidity has become oppressive. A pigeon flies cautiously at low level through the many trees, looking more like a lark than a pigeon. Two small children come through, very small. One of them has a large fishing net, which from the tip of the handle to the end of the hoop is larger than he is. Another little fellow, half his size, follows him. I ask if he is going fishing. He says, "No, I am going to catch birds."

A dramatic scene rises up as we come now to some tall cypress trees, one of which is broken off at the top and splintered in many pieces, and I wonder if that is the work of lightning also. I see no burn scars on it, but it is split right down the middle, and large pieces are lying on the ground. And as we come along, circling toward the west of the park, we come upon another tall cypress tree which has been split about twenty feet from the ground. The wood looks like giant, jagged splinters, frayed beyond recognition as a tree, almost as if it had been split into rails. This cypress is about the same circumference as the two standing nearby, which tower about sixty feet into the air. I inspect it closely for any signs of lightning, but can see none. Some powerful force splintered this tree, it almost looks like from within, because it branches out like a bunch of toothpicks placed loosely in a holder. The center is quite open as the wood fans out toward the top. Again we see the spectacular display of the forces of nature, in the stately old cypress tree and the bolt of lightning. Cypress trees are a favorite target of lightning because of their high moisture content.

In the pond, which was created as a boat pond, the children still try to catch minnows, which they take home and attempt to keep as pet fish. The concept that Shaw had of a pond to sail boats on, as they did in England, is interesting. He probably did not take into consideration that children in England, a maritime nation, might naturally be sailing boats. I don't know if anyone has sailed a boat on Tower Grove Pond, but I've never seen anyone sail a boat here. I remember, however, as a child, that some very elegant boats were available, and a school mate of mine had one of these. It was made of metal, and you could wind it up. The propeller would make it go for a long way on the pond. But I don't remember that we ever put it on a pond. My wife tells me that, yes, they did sail boats in the boat pond when she was a child, half a century ago.

The monkey-brained fruit of the Osage orange is bountiful on the ground now.

# The Park
# In Autumn

*"A tree is a monument which serves the birds of the air, the beasts of the field, and man."—James Gurney*

It is a Thursday in September, two days after the first day of Autumn. We are walking around an area by the Walking Road, in a line with the pond, where, last week, we saw hundreds of Monarch butterflies. Today there is not a single butterfly around the trees. Last week they were hanging from the branches like so many brown and orange leaves, swaying listlessly in the breeze as their wings slowly undulated. They are on their way south from as far north as Canada, and will winter in the Sierra Madre region of Mexico, and return north next year.

Although Autumn is officially here, there are no leaves changing in the park. As we move farther east, a Monarch butterfly flies by at the intersection of the Oak Hill path and the Walking Road. Another single butterfly goes by, but there are none in the trees.

By the Music Stand there are Osage orange fruits on the ground. They make good food for the birds, for as they gradually decay, the seeds are exposed. The Music Stand has a wire fence around it, and a sign saying "Keep Out." The floor has been replaced and a new prime coat of paint put on it. I am happy to see the Music Stand being maintained. Close by the ginkgo tree has dropped its fruit which smells strong, with a very disagreeable odor. By the boat pond there is a pyracantha bush full of orange berries. Another lone Monarch flies by.

*The Gatehouse at West Gate*

We walk in the wet grass across from the boat pond on a Saturday morning. The sun is shining, but I have a jacket on and it feels good. The week was an eventful one in the park. There was the migration of the Monarch butterflies, a wedding party posing for a photographer by the ruins near the boat pond, and last, the odor of the dropping ginkgo fruit. Now the catalpa trees are starting to look rather bare, their leaves turning yellowish green. The lady cigars, or seed pods, are very visible, giving a strange appearance to the trees which look, from the distance, like brown-bearded, gnarled gnomes.

On a Sunday in late September, the park is the setting for a neighborhood fair! There is a square dance group performing, boys and girls in pink and red costumes, moving gracefully to the music, while the caller sings out, "Do se do, don't you know, you'll never get to Heaven if you don't get a beau!"

We move over toward the stands where food is served to see what is offered. The menu includes: fried chicken, bar-be-qued beef, Italian sausage sandwiches, bakery goods, doughnuts, sausage and sauerkraut, American Indian fried bread, pork steak, Chinese food, egg roll, fried rice, fortune cookies, sweet-sour pork,—a more varied menu would be hard to find at any restaurant.

On the stage modern music is being played, and sung, by the Grand Fuzz, a group of young policemen, while everyone gathers around, munching and drinking and clapping hands. The carnival booths are enticing and offer a wide array of games of skill for which prizes are awarded: tic-tac-toe ball, tip the cat, bumper car, teddy bear toss, seven-eleven, bottle ring, and a dart game. Away from this area, but under the trees which offer protection from the sun, which is still warm in late September, are the numerous colorful, enticing booths of the flea market. The sellers are mostly amateurs with things dug up from basements, or hauled down from attics, with things made with their own hands, or purchased and decorated at home.

After the square dance we listen to the Grand Fuzz, we play the games, we chomp on sausages, fried bread, sweet-sour pork, and wash it down with cold drinks. Then we lie down on the grass and watch the people, who are the central theme in this early autumn festival. We relax in this delightful atmosphere of the park with people leisurely having fun.

The first Sunday in October, we are on the north side of the Main Drive, by the path that comes off Roger Place, an area we don't get into very often. The earth is soft under foot, from the rains we had last week. This path goes all the way across the park, and leads to a street, Thurmond Avenue. A little storage building stands nearby. The path connects up with a broad concrete walk about the width of three city sidewalks. There is a metal marker set in the concrete that says, "P.M. Bruner, Granitoid Co., St. Louis, Mo."

This is an interesting little entrance off of Thurmond Avenue, where the path from Roger Place ends up. You may want to explore it for yourself sometime. The entrance is flanked on one side by a large golden rain tree and on the other by a couple of red bud trees. Beyond the golden rain tree is a linden. This must be a very beautiful place in the Springtime.

Walking up the field on the Magnolia Street side, suddenly the Music Stand comes into view, through the clearing and the trees on the left. Halfway between me and the Music Stand is a large tree which has been split all the way down to the base. It may have been hit by lightning. I go over to take a closer look. No, it looks now like a part of the tree had, perhaps, a large branch on it, which rotted underneath and had fallen and split the tree down the side where there was a decayed streak running down. There are roots up there where the break was, as if some other tree had grown in there. A peculiar sight.

The painting of the Music Stand floor has been completed, a design in two colors of brown, light and dark, radiating from the center. Little parquets of wood on the edge, about eight of them, are painted red, making a very attractive design.

I just saw a young bearded man, with a number of leaves in his hand and a couple of books, examining leaves of a tree. A group of young children are going into the Music Stand, looking at the new floor. There's a man walking over to the statue of von Steuben. He has a topcoat on, the first one I've seen this season. Now he is examining the statue, reading the inscription on it.

The lilies are in bloom and the giant lily pads have some buds on them, which are enormous, about the size of large coconuts. One of them is in bloom, a gorgeous white, and very large.

There's a new beauty to the park this morning with the change of the season. Not that the leaves have changed that much, although a few have, but the feeling of the air and the position of the sun on the leaves has changed, giving a different color and shadows, different from Summer, making this a delightful place to be. There are several pyracantha bushes by the old ruins, and they are just ablaze with orange, a beautiful sight against the green. A big old elm broods over there, looking almost like a ghost, very sickly, withered leaves, not quite green and not quite brown, a spectral sight, but quite beautiful from across the pond.

Yesterday I talked to three young boys by the pond, who had roller skated over from Flora Place, about three blocks north, and they were warm and sweaty. It was a nice little skate and they were really dressed for it. They had on blue shoe skates, and stockings with some roller skating emblems on them, like a uniform. They were practicing for a roller derby which they want to enter. It was humid and we all complained about the mosquitoes.

The wind has died down and now I can feel the sun warming me through my jacket. I see an elderly lady walking down the path at the intersection of Main Drive and the Roger Place path, with her coat around her shoulders. She is wearing a hat and high heels, and I wonder if she is walking to Grand Avenue, perhaps to the Lutheran Church. That's a long walk, but what if it takes all morning on a Sunday? When one is older, one has time for such things. The little lady, well dressed, wearing glasses, is walking slowly, down the path. A boy is running with his dog. A camper and three cars are parked at the east end of the park. There's a man letting his police dog out of his car to run while he sits in the car with the motor running. By the Sons of Rest pavilion, which is now completely renovated, a big picnic is being set up on this cool October day. According to my estimate, the older lady has about a half mile to walk to the church.

Walking west on Arsenal Street on the park side I can look across the street at some of the buildings on the east end. I see a beautiful residence with a facade of fancy tiles and brick work. At another place, on the second floor, I see a little old lady in a wheel chair, looking out a curtainless window. I can't tell if she is looking out or just staring somewhere in the room. I feel loneliness seeing her there.

The architecture of these buildings is interesting. Many were built as large flats, a few as single family dwellings, but not all are built the same. The house on the corner of Roger and Arsenal has a kind of Swiss chalet motif with stucco and timber type construction of the walls. The stucco has not been painted for some time, which gives it a very nice appearance, sort of creamy yellow, an antique hue.

On a Saturday early in October we are walking down the south field, the long field, across from the boat pond. The leaves haven't changed very much yet. There are some yellows and the oaks have a bit of rouge on their cheeks. Here's a scarlet tree over here, and it's right in between two other green trees and makes a beautiful sight. I think it is a black gum tree. The one on the left is a horse chestnut, tinged with red a little bit, and the tree on the right is a linden, still green. Here are some pretty red and yellow leaves on the gum tree, just starting out. A portly young man is looking at the statue of von Steuben. That makes two weeks in a row I've seen someone looking at that statue. The big Amazon water lilies havent bloomed any more. It may be a bit too chilly.

It's a cool crisp Sunday morning, cloudy with the sun trying to break out. There's a crew cutting down a dead elm, just west of the Chinese gazebo, and I am surprised to see them working on a Sunday morning. In the area where I did the Winter walk, I look forward to doing it again. We scarcely missed a week end last Winter even with all the snow.

The leaves are falling now, red leaves, and yellow from the poplars. I think as we walk through these nice little parts of the park, that we need to emphasize the appreciation of such environments. If we only think of parks in terms of sports and other types of activities, rather than aesthetics, then we won't have strolling parks. This park is probably one of the rare examples of such a park in existence today.

Again I see the lady who was walking here last Sunday, with the coat around her shoulders, and she has come to the part of the path where the tree is being cut down. She had to walk all around the bushes there, walking through the grass in the mud. The branches are piled on the path, and although the branches are small, they are just enough to keep a well dressed person from trying to get through. Now the lady is sitting down on the bench, resting.

Here's an oak tree, reddish-brown. A man walking through the park with a paper under his arm, evidently has been somewhere else and is carrying the paper back with him through the park. Five crows are sitting under a tree, sitting in a circle, talking about something, no doubt.

Perhaps betting odds on the football game today, or maybe they have a crow game.

On a Saturday in the middle of October the sky is overcast with light rain falling off and on. The wind is blowing up now and then, and we come to look at the leaves changing. Some leaves are turning red, the pin oaks. Here's a big old tree turning yellow. It has oval leaves. I don't know what kind of a tree it is. I haven't noticed it before. Could it be a shagbark hickory? It's a beautiful tree with the branches hanging down, all clear underneath, making a protective bower. It's right next to the smaller gazebo that's in line with the statue of von Humboldt.

Over by the big "King Oak," which has just turned a little bit red and brown, I notice that while walking in the park I can sing. I can sing to myself, and I do now. No one to bother me. You very seldom hear people singing to themselves in the park, except in movies.

The pyracantha bushes by the boat pond stand out in their orange beauty. There are quite a few lilies out yet. It's amazing with the frost we had. The Amazon lilies are still budding, and one of them is trying to burst out. I think it will make it.

It is starting to rain again, and we'll have to head back. Herb likes to walk around the edges of the concrete pond, like a little kid. I've never walked the whole park in one day, but will some day. Around the von Humboldt statue, two nice maples are starting to turn, contrasting green and yellow. Another tree has been cut down. There will be many cut down this year. At the Columbus statue the pavilion is looking good. There's an oak, big and beautiful with russet coloring. The ginkgoes are just beginning to turn yellow. In one night they may all shed their leaves. In the shadow, I see some trees turning a very dark red.

It is a Friday evening in late October, a beautiful Fall day. There are many people sitting around the boat pond. The late afternoon light is filtering through the trees, and the back lighting looks like a photographer's dream. The temperature is eighty degrees. An Osage orange tree's leaves have turned yellow, and another next to it is still green. A couple of oak trees are brownish orange. Over in the south field it is beautiful with the sunlight on the trees turning the changing color of the leaves different shades of green, yellow, orange, and red. More people are out than I have seen in quite a while. The warm temperature and the colors must attract them.

Saturday morning, in the center of the park, at the Cypress Circle, with the pine trees and the cypress, I see a very large grove of poplar trees all turned yellow. It's cloudy but warm. Here's a group of birch trees, mostly green tinged with a little of yellow. It's quiet this morning with very few people. One car just went through and there is one car by the boat pond. Here is a group of beautiful trees, just west of the Chinese gazebo. Another oak, broader leaf than the pin oak, is more brown than red. A big maple, which I remember from the time when a friend took pictures for me when I first started the walking guide, is a beautiful golden yellow. The yellow of the poplars is bright against the dark green of the pine trees. There are very pretty poplar trees just a little south of the druid circle. There is some life in the park now, a girl walking through, wearing a heavy blouse, evidently using the park as a short cut. Two dobermans are running loose with their master; a cyclist is passing through, time about 9:30 a.m. Some bushes have turned a brilliant red by the Chinese gazebo, with an orange and yellow background. A whole row of ginkgoes have turned yellow. In the Cypress Circle, big cypress are surrounded by pines. It is difficult to realize from outside the traffic circle that in the center are these gigantic cypress trees, beautiful columns of living wood, stretching into the sky. Looking to the northwest from the Cypress Circle the colors are intriguing.

Near the east entrance there's a pungent smell in the air on a Sunday morning. I don't know how to describe it. It is related to the smell of mushrooms and may be from all the leaves on the ground. I see some gum trees, all shades of yellow and red, and next to them one that hasn't changed yet at all. At the Sons of Rest shelter now, the roof newly painted, a table is overturned. South and east of the shelter is a very nice woods, a very pleasant feeling woods, just the kind of thing you want to walk into, very inviting. I guess the nice thing about it is that you walk into the different colors, from orange to yellow to red, and there is a different kind of light in each tree, The sun is barely shining this morning. There's the big old poplar tree with the hole in its side. Here is a grove of pin oaks, just medium sized trees, and there's exactly a dozen of them. The arrangements of the plantings are fantastic here. There's a maple that hasn't changed yet.

Going out now to the south field at the east end, there's that smell in the air again, an earthy smell, as if coming from the ground. The fallen leaves are starting to decay. A couple with a dog on a leash are walking through. Here's a father with three children, playing in the grass over by Arsenal Street where their Volkswagon bus is parked. Walking west I top the knoll at Spring Avenue and see a beautiful view to the west, the field and all the different colored trees on the edges. It's really an impressive sight, the only distraction being the soccer field in the middle with its goal posts. Over by the Chinese gazebo is one of my favorite areas in Fall, because the colors of the gazebo, red, green, and gold, blend nicely with the various colors of the leaves. To the north and south you have the dark green background of the conifers, with squirrels all around, and stately pin oaks of indescribable beauty.

Here is one of the most beautiful scarlet trees I have seen in the park. It is on the north vehicular drive at the east end, by the curve with the bridge. I identified it as a black gum, which turns red early in the Fall. Not far from it is a magnificent gum tree, red and yellow and green.

It is the first part of November now, the end of Fall, and there are not many leaves left on the trees, mostly green and yellow leaves, not nearly as colorful as earlier. The leaves on the ground rustle as Herb and I walk through them, and I like to listen to the differences in sound patterns between Herb's four-legged shuffling and my two-legged shuffling through the leaves. There are some people in the park, but no one walking at 8:30 a.m.

It's a cloudy and cool morning, not nippy, but just cool. There's a kind of lingering warmth from Summer yet, even in November, like a mantle of air rather than a wet blanket. Some ginkgoes have shed their leaves. Here's one over here by the "King Oak." It's really pretty, because there's green all around on the ground and this carpet of gold forms a circle around the tree. An unusual sight. Here's another one with a carpet of brown leaves, and the golden leaves sprinkled in between, making colorful lawn decorations here in the park today. The old "King Oak" still has its leaves, sort of a rusty brown. A few more people are appearing in the park, a man with a couple of dogs, some runners, a cyclist.

The park is particularly attractive in the Fall when many of the trees are bare and there are a few with leaves. Walking along the paths, on the south side, going around the traffic circle with the statue of von Humboldt, there is a gazebo on the right, the statue on the right ahead, a gazebo on the left, and a gazebo up ahead. As you walk along the curving path you can see all this at the same time. There are delights of the eye in the late Fall and the Winter that you will not be granted in the Summertime when heavy foliage obscures them. I don't know when I like the park the most. I sort of like it better in Winter, when it is alone in all its splendor, and I am alone with it, rather than in the Summer when it is filled with leaves and people. But perhaps those are two aspects of the same thing, a going apart and a coming together, the rhythm of the seasons and of Man. What if Death were like Autumn? Would it be more bearable? Coming slowly and with beauty, and a gradual decline that speaks of Old Age? If that were Death, ending then in bareness and a promise, of the Spring, could one walk into Death like a park?

Another cloudy, coolish early November Sunday morning, but not too cool. I've got a sweater and a rain coat on. It feels good. I have the feeling about November that I had yesterday. Here's a bare tree, a large one, with its gracefully arching branches. It's a poplar tree, and has some of the old blossoms still on it, a very pretty tree, and you can see it in all its strength and beauty in the Wintertime.

Strange, here is a large tulip poplar. Evidently the weather is warm enough, and it has started to bud again. There are little green buds on the ends of the twigs, and absolutely no leaves on the tree. Here's a batch of really interesting mushrooms, in clumps, and they have a trumpet like shape, with broad gills. They look like *coprinus* or inky caps. That's what they must be, as some of them have already melted into a black oozing liquid. These mushrooms have been here awhile as they are in a state of advanced decay. We've had almost a week of rain, and the moisture has brought out a lot of mushrooms. I saw some in a cemetery this week. They looked like Destroying Angel of the *amanita* species.

There were two women out here gathering the fruit of the ginkgo trees, a big pail full of them. I asked the one woman if they made something out of them and she nodded her head, "Yes." She didn't speak. I asked if they were used for cooking, and she again nodded her head, "Yes."

The middle of November in Tower Grove Park across from the boat pond it is a beautiful morning in November, crisp, cool with the sun up. There is a kind of bright crystal clear sunlight bouncing off the stones of the ruins by the pond. The sunlight glancing off those stones is so white and bright, just about as snappy as the air itself. The grass is up nice and green, with the moisture we have had these past few weeks. There is a big gum tree by the boat pond, full of leaves and still full of color, red and brown near the top and green and yellow sprinkled with brown in the lower part. It is hard to describe this November sun. There is something about it that is so bright and white. It changes the color of everything. Looking at the grass in that light, it is a different color than it is in the Summertime. You cannot see sunlight at home, bricked in, as you can in the park, reminding you, in its slanting lines, of a day you loved, or a love you knew.

There are a few people here this morning. One car is parked down the road, by the first traffic circle. There's a fellow jogging down the Walking Road. I saw four older men in the park this morning; three were in cars and one was walking. Two got out of their cars and walked. I talked to the one man walking his dog, which is thirteen years old. He said she has trouble with her teeth, has heart murmur, and that it costs more to take care of a dog, medically, than a human.

The day before Thanksgiving Day is a chilly and moist day. It rained early this morning and we have a dark November sky with the sun kind of palely piercing through here and there. A great November morn before Thanksgiving.

This morning I imagine that Herb is the master and I am the dog, following him. I bark occasionally and follow wherever he leads me. I bark rather well, I think, for a human. He goes to some very stupid places, as the dog that I am is a man-dog and not a dog-dog.

We are coming to the end of the Fall season and there are a few green leaves still on the trees here and there. Still a slight vestige of the fullness of Summer, even though it is the day before Thanksgiving. But many of the trees are bare. A row of long, slender ginkgoes along the drive attest to that, and their dark slender bodies seem to try to pierce the gloom of the overhanging November sky without success.

The Chinese gazebo is revealed completely now, no leaves of trees to hide its beauty, setting there among a clump of bushes with red leaves on them, complementing very well its red and gold roof. Up close the gazebo looks even more beautiful. The plantings certainly do complement it.

I am in the Cypress Circle, filled with cypress and pine, and I am shocked to realize for the first time, that these cypress trees lose their leaves in the Winter. It doesn't seem right somehow. They should be evergreen

On Thanksgiving Day we return to the Chinese gazebo, strikingly beautiful with its surrounding red shrubbery, red and gold roof and green columns underneath a somber, grey sky and bare trees. There is no one else here in the park this morning except for two men joggers on the Walking Road and one woman jogger on the path along the Main Drive. Herb is kicking up his hind legs in a pile of dead leaves. Nippy and cold this morning, moist, the kind of cold that gets to your ear and nose tips very readily. I wish I had put my cap on.

Back up again by the clump of new birches, looking nice with some yellow leaves still on them. Coming over to the little stone bridge with the triangular caps on it, I smell the great smells of Fall, the smell now of a cut oak, an odor that is sometimes pleasant, sometimes unpleasant, depending on how strong it is. But the smells of Fall are certainly around us, if you add the smell of cut oak to the smell of dead leaves, crumpled up and being shredded by many people walking over them, perhaps some mowing and mulching also, it gives that distinct, moist smell of decline, the smell of Fall.

There's a tree here that is just full of yellow leaves, and everything behind it is bare and black. A beautiful sight, an unusual sight, and one that could only be glimpsed by coming through here at this time of year. On

closer examination the tree turns out to be a maple, one of the few that still has leaves on it.

Looking through the druid circle of trees, there are still a few trees through the way that have yellow leaves, and beyond some red bushes far off through the distance. By the Sons of Rest shelter there are many cars parked, probably people going to the Thanksgiving Day services at the Lutheran Church.

I am really chilled now, having walked about fifteen minutes, and starting to feel the cold around my head, my nose and my eyes. Crossing over Main Drive, just west of the Columbus statue, walking toward the octagon-shaped gazebo, one of the most exquisite small gazeboes in the park, I see now the stumps of two large trees, and they seem to have been very solid trees, about two feet in diameter. Probably had elm disease. We come across the remains of a dead rabbit or squirrel. I can't tell which, perhaps a rabbit. As we approach the gazebo, pigeons are walking around the brick floor. The temperature is thirty-eight degrees.

The day after Thanksgiving, a very chilly overcast sky, the wind blowing, which will bring some colder weather with it. Forecast of light snow this afternoon, and cold weather over the weekend. Here's a dog running loose, kind of an airdale type. A group of kids are playing soccer.

At the east end of the park, a little east of the Chinese gazebo, there's one tree here in a row of trees, that still has its green leaves. They have not turned color in any way, but are green, and have started to wither now as green leaves and some of them have fallen off the tree, still green, and are lying on the ground. It's a linden tree. Maybe we can learn a lesson from this tree that stays green until the end of November. If we can stay green that long too!

"Pigeons on the grass alas, alas. Pigeons on the grass alas!" Gertrude Stein would love this park. The pigeons are here in abundance. They seem to be feeding under some seed trees. We pass now under a giant poplar tree, and next to it a huge ginkgo, all bare, and walk into the druid circle, right into the middle of it. Yellow leaves scat-

60

tered all over the ground from a maple tree, shedding late. It may be the one I saw the other day with all of its leaves still on. They all fell at one time. The wind is cold now blowing up against me. I don't want to stop. Herb does and I think he is cruel keeping me out in this chilly weather.

Wheee! Ooooouee! The leaves are rolling along the ground with a November tumble that makes you know that things are hurrying along, that time is moving and that you're not moving with it. That feeling, that November feeling that is hard to shake, when the cold wind comes into your bones.

Now, there's a runner, in shorts, on the Walking Road. We are in a heavily wooded area, just east of the wooden bridge on the Walking Road. A beautiful wood for November, or a wood for Winter, a wood for darkness, heavy, heavy feeling of November, especially towards the end.

The November scene is a revealing one, things being revealed that were hidden before, things that are the fruits of Spring, Summer, and Fall. Bristly pine cones, prickly gum balls from the gum trees, seed pods from the tulip poplar, and dried leaves. November is a time of show and tell. It's a time for reflection, a time before Winter, a very special time, a time in between, and times in between are always very special. November is what's left after the full and bountiful harvest, it's what remains after all that Man would gather is gone. November sums it up for Nature, saying this is Me, after you have taken what you want away. November is a woman.

# The Park
# In Winter

*"Flowers and trees preach grander, deeper and more eloquent sermons than all the ministers."*—James Gurney

The wide, white expanse of snow is impressive with brown leaves, and little tufts of green grass sticking up here and there. And the trees, once again, are a predominant feature, with their black faces staring at you blankly, almost questioning your intrusion on this sacred scene, in which they, as permanent residents and guardians of the park, preside with silent dignity.

Overnight, the full evergreens have sprouted fluffy white blossoms of snow, I glance off to the right and see the iron-work humped back bridge and the stone bridge next to it. Without any movement, without any cars, without any people, one thinks naturally of a pristine world, of a new world, an unspoiled world, of an uncluttered world, where the very movement of life itself is still, and the great movement of life which Man has given it, quieted.

Under some of the trees there are pock marks like on the moon, where snow has fallen off the branches and made imprints on the ground snow. The wind is blowing the snow in sheets from the gazebo roofs and pelts us with miniature snowballs. Under a large oak I am showered with white powder.

As we approach the humped-back metal scroll bridge, I notice that there are no human tracks other than my own, and that there are little squiggly lines of animal tracks here and there. My dog, Herb, sniffs the snow anxiously, trying to smell through the hard crust which is underlain with ice this morning, to get the scent of a burrowing mole.

We walk past the first range of trees and as I turn to look at them, they present to me their white stippled sides, which have borne the brunt of the icy wind and snow during the night, and their long faces are highlighted by the night's wintry cosmetic that lined their features with white and frosted their coiffures.

Crossing over one drive we go back to the bridge on the other side, wallowing in the lonely pleasure of trammeling untrodden snow. There are two huge trees to the right of me that beckon with grotesque branches lined with white powder. But we do not follow, for Herb has found a scent and burrowed under the snow and ice to the wet fresh ground and now drags me this way and that in pursuit of his quarry.

We pass by the statue of Alexander von Humboldt, and he has a shawl of white about his coat, extending down the arms, and a silly-looking, riduculous white skull cap and white toes on his shoes. Having Alexander looking so stately, almost every day, this Winter caricature strikes me as very funny, and I laugh out loud in the emptiness of the park. He looks very much like a freshman pledge for a fraternity, following his initiation rite in the park.

We return again to the path, and I see a large bird come in to the drinking fountain. It is a black crow, blacker yet against the snow, looking for a drink. He seems to wait patiently and finds some water. I see him drink, hold up his beak and let the water run down. As I approach I notice that the bubbler is still bubbling and the crow enjoyed a morning drink from the human fountain which has been inadvertently provided him, without competition from man. I approach now myself, and see what a haven it is in Winter for birds as the bubbler runs and the water runs, and there is a pool of water in the iron basin, and the water flows into the ground to a small creek nearby. We go over to see where the water flows out, and indeed it is trickling and not frozen, but the water above is frozen. Herb runs across it, but I jump rather than risk getting a foot wet.

Approaching us, we see a solitary figure, a neatly dressed, trim old man, in a pea coat and black knit hat. He says, "Nice Day!" and we say, "Yes, isn't it!" Each of us seemed surprised to see the other. And from his walk, as I regard him in passing, I think that he is an old sailor, who has walked this way many times.

We walk now rather aimlessly, here and there, heading in the direction of the gazeboes, and I find it intriguing trying to note exactly where I am, having to study the paths and the roads covered with snow now, and look at the landmarks, the gazeboes and trees, and their new relationships without the pointing of the paths. And an entirely different world is created in which the gazeboes have a life of their own and a marking of their own and a claim on the land, aside from cars, and paths, and roads. And I come upon the huge "King Oak" and note how its crotches are laden with snow, and how it stands mute and inscrutable, with its many knotted eyes peering at me, saying "I am the King. I am the mightiest of oaks in the park. See how my branches hold the snow. See how I lift them up to be viewed by God alone."

The snowfall is not a heavy one, but is a crunchy one, and it is cold. It is a firm one with ice beneath, that speaks of Winter, that says, "Yes, I am the Winter snow. I cover the ground and hold it fast, for the time of my life." And I walk away from the park, hoping that I can cling to my earth with such fondness and tenacity, for the time of my life.

I am walking on the Main Drive at the east end of the park, near the blue-gray gazebo, which I think can be best appreciated in the Winter. You can see it at a distance then through the trees, and if you are at the Chinese gazebo you can see the pale blue ghost of the frail, delicate gazebo from the distance. And it is a rare sight, because you can only do this in the Winter, the rest of the year the view being obscured by the leaves of the trees. This is a particularly delightful gazebo to enjoy, and I guess I would have to say it is my favorite if forced to make the choice. Looking at it from a distance, then walking toward it is a rather unique experience, because you see this ghostlike structure, almost like an apparition in the sunlight, and you are naturally attracted toward it like a magnet. As you walk toward it, it begins to take form and shape and the delicateness of the arches and the woodwork and the sides of the gazebo begin to appear, and suddenly you are there, and it is there in all its full beauty. It is just a delight to look at and behold on a rather pleasant, warmish Winter morning.

It's a Monday in late December and I am on the path by Roger Place and Arsenal Street in a grove of Osage orange trees, looking eastward toward the playing field, near three other Osage orange trees which are close to a bench. Those trees, along with two hackberry trees to the south of them, present a very grotesque scene to me, for some reason, this morning. Their limbs are curved, twisted in many different directions. I notice now that the limbs of the Osage orange tend to bend toward those of the hackberry, and those of the hackberry towards those of the Osage orange. It's almost as if they were beckoning together, with those crooked gnarled fingers of their limbs, for me to approach this playing field, where there are dozens of the Osage orange fruits, or monkey-brains, as the kids call them. Perhaps there is a game to be played in the Winter time that none of us knows about, and if we could somehow communicate with these venerable trees, with their playing equipment which they create from their own life sap, perhaps, we could learn a new game to play with the trees, and the fields and the fruit of the trees. As I stand here looking at them, and the playing field with its goals, I think of how we are barricaded from experiencing some of the things we might experience because of such barriers as the playing goals which put us into a particular categorical frame of mind. And we think, yes, it is a soccer game. That is what is played here now. Or maybe some touch football. So, perhaps, we shall never know the game to which the Osage orange and the hackberry trees are beckoning us, and we will live in our ignorance and miss a great deal of experience.

As I think these thoughts I wonder about Winter thoughts. Are Winter thoughts different than Summer thoughts? Or Autumn thoughts? I think they are. We think different things and feel different things in the various seasons of the year. It's one of the reasons we long for one season over the other. We feel these things, and speak these things because of the differences in the seasons.

Just west of the Chinese gazebo a big tree is cut down and a smaller one. That is a large old tree. What kind it is I do not know, but it's like two trees growing together. It is immense. The bark comes off easily. Perhaps it is a dead elm. Here's a smaller one. Some big old trees are here yet. The old hackberry, I hope, is here. Yes, with all its inscriptions, and the big old oak next to it, are still remaining, beautiful specimens of trees.

The wind is coming up now. It was pleasant before without the wind. The temperature is in the mid-twenties, maybe going up toward thirty. But when the wind blows straight into your face, it's not pleasant, really. Herb continues to walk, regardless of the weather.

Two days after Christmas I am on the south side of the park, west of the traffic circle, in a little forest of trees. I notice how the shadows seem to fall softly across me as I walk by the trees, and it is a nice feeling of the sunlight and the shadows. It kind of embraces me. Makes me feel good. And that is one of the things you must learn in life, what makes you feel good, and pursue those things in some fashion, on some pattern, in order to round out your life, otherwise you'll always be feeling bad.

Part of the problem, I think, we have in modern life is not simply a matter of not having enough time, but being able to make the transitions from one mode of brain activity to another. We are in a rational, linear task and suddenly we want to move to another mood, and we walk in the park, but we don't enjoy it because we are still in the rational, linear mode. And we need little rituals to shift gears. Not just walking through the sunlight and shadows of the trees here, but thinking about that, and getting a feeling of how that sunlight and shadow feels on you, is, for me, and possibly for you, a little ritual of transition from one moment to the next. I can walk out and feel refreshed, rather than simply being in this new environment, a lovely environment, such as Tower Grove Park, and staying in my old mood which takes away from me some of the enjoyment and beauty that I should be experiencing.

On the last day of the year in Tower Grove Park it is just below the freezing mark. There's heavy moisture in the air, a mist, occasionally some rain, and a light fog, more like a haze, pervades the park, giving it a kind of dream-like atmosphere, a landscape effect that is very enchanting despite the chilly, wet weather. I do not know why I come to the park on a morning like this except it be for Herb whose enthusiasm knows not the changes of climate or weather. And certainly without his enthusiasm for being in the park, which I somehow share with him, I wouldn't be here. The air has the smell of wet, cold iron, as if foretelling that the heavy hammer of Winter is about to fall.

Today is the day after a great ice storm in the city and the park bears the marks of the icy visitor, almost like a monster from outer space, who has transformed the land-scape into bizarre shapes, especially the trees and shrubs, and under foot has laid down a glaze of ice on which to slip and slide, for one can scarcely keep one's footing on the icy ground.

I dig the heels of my boots into the frosted ground to keep a footing and avoid the pavement paths where there's no resilience to the step. But here, Herb and I can roam safely, though precariously, as long as we remember to dig in. Sometimes Herb forgets to extend his claws and slips along with surprising speed and amazes even himself in his fleet-footed run through the park.

Now let's see what this icy monster, who was swept in on the jet stream, from god knows where, (it may well have been outer space) has done. His bizarre touch is apparent everywhere. He has magically turned gazeboes into ice palaces, where no one dwells, amid a cold beauty that no one sees, except a few fool-hardy explorers like Herb and myself, for I have seen no other living thing in the park. We could easily be with Admiral Byrd at the North Pole, so desolate is the scene before us. Except that now we have stumbled upon a magic kingdom unknown to any-one, a beautiful land of fairy-like structures, decorated with icicles of all shapes and descriptions. From the Music Stand and from the Turkish pavilion, the small gazeboes and large, lovely, symmetrical, long, cool, transparent icicles cling in rows like a line of irregular troops, hastily mustered volunteers, called to defend their country. They hang there now, defying us to break into their solitude, to cross the barriers, for they just might reward us with a fat hunk of ice on the head, or perhaps trick us into falling on an icy threshold to the entrance of their realm.

But then as I approach the Sons of Rest shelter, I see that the ice-monster has decorated it in a different, more frivolous mood, and I am reminded of the frozen custard stands of the 1930's which had plaster icicles with glitter on them, and I expect at any moment to see a plaster statue of a polar bear throwing a snowball, since they were the beasts commonly chained to those delectable ice cream stands, so that they would not be taken from their hoary habitat by eager animal collectors. But there are no polar bears, no bears at all, no animals, nothing to shake the illusion that we are still in a magical frozen kingdom. How I long to see some form of life. A delightful horse and sleigh coming down the old carriage road would be a welcome sight. And my mind carries me to the land of my mother's childhood and the delightful stories she told about the great winters in the Austrian Alps, when the snow was so high they could not get out of their houses. And I wonder, does that land still live; do the horses and sleighs still run? I must go there soon and find out.

And when the land was out of Winter's grip, she said, then they would take the cows up into the mountains, where the cows grazed for the Summer, returning in Autumn, at the time of the feast, Oktober Fest, when bonfires burned for their return. And I remember, now, the voice of my mother, yodeling. When I was small I thought, how unusual to have a mother who could yodel. None of my friends had mothers who could yodel. But my mother could yodel. And we even had phonograph records, the cylinder kind, on which other people yodeled. But no one, no one, I ever met, after that, could yodel.

So with memories of my yodeling mother trailing from my brain, I walk with Herb the simple path that the park had transformed into magic and fantasy. I thought, what a treasure to have such a place, a public place, that one could go to be transformed. And then it was that I realized what the park is for many people, a place beyond simple ball playing, running, jumping, or even trees, flowers and shrubs, but for us who must dwell in the city, it is a place where our souls might go and wander at will with absolute freedom. Eat your heart out Carlos Castaneda.

Ice fingers trace ice dreams across a winter sky, entering elegant descriptions of Winter for our audience now. They stretch from every cupola, from every arch and post, beckoning, enticing to stay within the Winter dream and leave behind the mundane world of bricks and mortar which we know is real. And here we can begin again with nothingness of snow that mutes the voice and chills the bone while beguiling us with white, blank pages for the ice fingers writing in the sky.

Have you ever felt the deadening insulation of three feet of snow? Walking over its crust the foot-speared wounds are muffled far below. It's difficult to walk and see, the snow is piled so deep, rising high about the trees it has climbed and perched on peaks. Perilous, now, we make our way unbidden and uncalled. Before us lies the vast expanse of Winter.

As I look out ahead I expect to hear the strains of "Somewhere My Love" and see a trans-Siberian railway express ploughing through the snow towards me. Stopping at this unlikely station, "The Music Stand," or the "Sons of Rest," whatever station you choose, the train would be equally at home. I would not bat an eyelash to see it stop and snort and start again and flash snow splashes from the rails. There are ten stations here in Gazeboland where my imaginary train might arrive and I can stop at any one of them and be assured of a ride.

The ice storm has taxed the trees heavily, many of them bending way over under the weight of the ice, limbs creaking, the squeal of ice sliding against ice. One thinks of icebergs in the north Atlantic with the sound of the squealing trees as the ice burdens them to their knees. And you wonder how they will be able to recover, and here and there you will see that branches have fallen and others are splitting under the tremendous weight of the ice imposed on the barren trees. Since the rain fell and then froze on to whatever it struck, the ice coating is thick and glazed. It is almost as if the trees were sculptured out of ice by some gigantic chef, preparing for a mighty feast of the gods, presenting a pretty confection of ice to refresh an Olympian eye, jaded with everyday scenes of the seasons it created.

It is the twelfth day of February, Lincoln's birthday, and it has been raining steadily all night, which comes right after the Spring thaw, after over 40 days of continuous snow cover. Although it is not raining presently, the sky is overcast, a medium brightness, not too much gloom, and the moisture and the warming has brought the smells of the organic materials out, and I walk through a dense cover of fallen leaves and their aroma comes up to me and of course brings the promise of Spring. This is an excellent time to come to the park to see the transition between Winter and Spring, and it just hangs there, almost hanging in the air as it were, in that aroma, in those smells that carry the promise. The moles have been busy under the cover of snow and there are a number of burrows pushing up all over. And Herb is inspecting some, but not very diligently for one who has been denied that pleasure so long because of the snow cover.

We come to what is the mid-point of Walk Two, I believe, and cross over to the Walking Road with the wooden railing on the bridge, and there stands the three-trunked tree, and some debris, some vegetable debris from the animals who have been working on something like an Osage orange, and some human debris, a beer can and a cola can and a smashed soda bottle on the road.

It is interesting that around the base of almost every tree along this road there is more of this vegetable debris, which looks like the fruit of the Osage orange, and I am trying to find out how it occurs. It looks like it may have dropped out of the trees, but on the other hand, these are different kinds of trees. None of them are Osage orange. Could the squirrels have carried the large Osage orange fruit up the trees? Not likely. But I am sure someone knows the answer. It is just another one of those things that you see and wonder about, coming into the park at different seasons of the year.

We cross back over to the main road and the foot bridge. On the other side is a clump of white birch, very attractive, which look like they were planted not too long ago, like a couple of years, and it may indicate some change in the types of trees which will be in Tower Grove Park. I had targeted to walk toward the little gazebo which is a twin to the one across the road, at the point of the traffic circle where the pines grow thick. But Herb's inclination has been otherwise, and I find myself much closer to my point of origin.

Standing at this point, I turn around to see a beautiful pin oak with branches, many branches, and they are all growing out at about the same angle of 45 degrees, a very beautiful tree in the Winter without any leaves. And on the side here I see an Osage orange tree, perhaps the source of the material I have been finding at the bases of the trees. Herb is now going "gung ho," having found a circle of mole runs and is digging them up, hopefully helping the appearance of grass in those spots in the Spring.

What happened here near the road is that some large gum trees have shed their seeds, and they look recent, because they are not decomposed. It may be that they were shed during the long Winter freeze and were preserved. Now they are almost in pristine condition, and if anyone is saving gum tree seeds for Christmas decorations, this would be an excellent place to gather them. I tried to gather some before Christmas, but had difficulty finding them, because, apparently, after they fall they decompose rapidly and lose much of their star-like effect, created by points and holes, very detailed and distinct, which makes them attractive. With time they become rather blunt and the holes are almost non-existent. So you have to get them fairly fresh after they fall if you want them for decorations.

There are still patches of snow on the ground. They are almost all gone now. The rain has pretty well eliminated them. There are some large patches here and there, not so much in the woods, but mostly in the open fields.

As life passes, so too with Winter. We stroll the park now on a day that appears to be the end of a very severe Winter. There has been almost record snowfall this year. The snow has been on the ground almost continuously for over sixty days. It is piled high in the park and everywhere else, but for the past two days there have been temperatures above freezing, so now the snow is melting fast. This is the Winter, the classic Winter, the Winter we knew of old, the Winter that our grandparents talked about when we thought it was cold, the kind of Winter that makes of Spring the return of a lost and lovely child.

So the mighty snow piles are beginning to melt, the pools of water are forming, the air is moist and cold. It is the end of Winter as we know it. It is the end of chills, of pains, and of aches in the back from lack of exercise. And muscles no longer are contracted but flex with the season.

Must Winter die? A pine tree branch, still green lies torn on the ground. It is beginning to rain. Must Winter die? Yes. As Summer fades, and Autumn dies into Winter, it too, itself, must die, and this, which we are witnessing today, is the death of Winter. We shall watch its final death throes, its passing, its joys, its regrets, its sorrows. And we come now past the gazebo with the cupola, towards the big "King Oak," which has stood here silently throughout the long Winter watch, and glance for the last time, perhaps, at the black sentinel trees against the white snow, and say, "Must this pass too?" To where do they go from here, from living death into life? Or is death their life, more so than Spring? We pass quietly, and with wonder, the great "King Oak."

Winter is a force that binds me to the path, as I cannot walk through the heavily drifted snow which is now soft and treacherous with porous moisture. Winter holds me here and there, in places that are warm and familiar. It beckons to adventure and wilderness, but I do not go. I stay beside the fire. Is it age, or is it wisdom?

Where does Winter go? It goes into the ground, forcing the worm to surface; it sinks in pools of snowy water around the trunks of trees, enabling them to come forth. It melts away into a frosty stream that freshens the rivers. It clings to the earth in desperation before the warmness of another season.

What is this Winter then, that dwelt so long among us? What kind of thing is it that held us in so long? Is Winter the oppressive tyrant of our childish dreams? Is Winter the binder to the earth that colors all our tales of death? Is Winter that last drama that completes the annual ritual cycle in which all of us must play? Or is Winter our lost memory of things that might have been?

Perhaps it was all of this, when first it started out, but now, as Winter dies, it takes on a different face. It is a giving. It is a sorrow. But it is Winter that is in sorrow. It is his. If November is a woman, then Winter is a man whose strength has waned. Winter is a play that's not been finished. As death dies, it casts no more shadow, but silently slinks into the ground, without ceremony, or ritual, to note that it has been here. Such rites are saved for Spring. Winter appears more the devil and can never be god. Man mourns not Winter like the other seaons, except for the few joys and sports it may provide. But we are glad to see him die, and so retell what mischief he has caused, how inconsiderate, how unkind, and we look forward to the Spring.

And, at the end, Winter weeps openly, his tears rolling from the cheeks of statues, dropping from the eaves of shelters, dripping from the limbs of trees, as I stand here by his death bed, wondering why I miss him. At last his frozen tears betray him, and he melts, not with pity, but with despair. A dying god, king Winter, lies supine upon a bed of muddy earth, moistened with his tears, the taste of salt and iron on his tongue.

# The Walks In Tower Grove Park

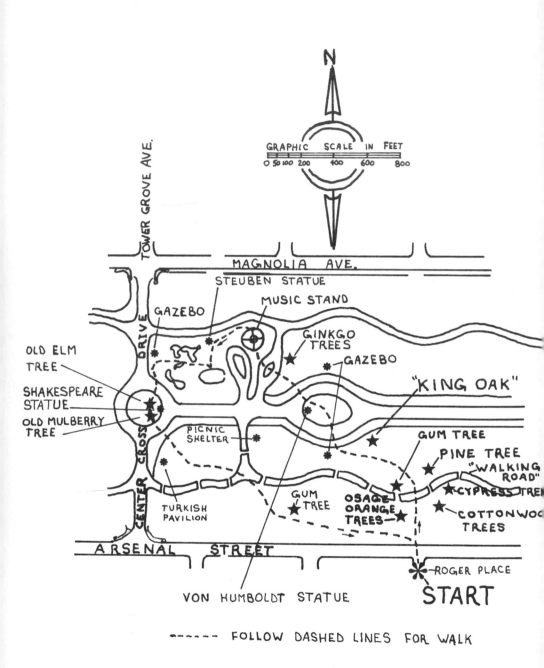

Walk 1 — The Central Area

# The First Walk

*"The Best way is to walk—to ramble through the pleasant scenes, making detours to right and left, as occasion may require."*
David H. MacAdam, "Tower Grove Park", 1883

There are many possible ways to enter Tower Grove Park. My favorite, by far, is to walk in at the informal entrance off Roger Place and Arsenal Street and take the well-worn, beaten and patched gravel-topped foot path past some shrubs and trees at the entrance. Once past the shrubs, look to the right and within about a hundred feet or so you will see a large cottonwood tree with extensive branches of unusual shape and size. There is a smaller cottonwood a little closer in, also on the right hand side. Now look both to the right and the left and take in the sweeping vistas provided by the open field, so characteristic of the English parks which Henry Shaw emulated in his design of Tower Grove Park. On the return leg of this walk you will have an opportunity to walk down the center of one of these fields and enjoy the sumptuous views and appreciate the fine design of the landscaping that is found throughout the park.

About a hundred yards farther down the path, on the left, notice some very large Osage orange trees. These venerable native trees with orangish brown bark form a protective bower of low lying branches in which the children love to hide and play. The fruit of the tree, which may be observed in the Fall, is about the size of a large orange and has a bright green convoluted surface which looks something like a brain. Children sometimes refer to them as "monkey brains."

*Gum Tree Leaves*

About fifty yards farther along the path you will come to a red graveled road which is closed to vehicular traffic and serves as a nice broad path. We will call it the "Walking Road." On the right, at the juncture of the path and the road, is a row of cypress trees, tall and narrow with feather-like leaves. On the other side of the road, after you walk just a few feet, discover a single pine tree with an unusual "S" shaped trunk. Across the road on the left is a medium-sized gum tree, which in the Fall displays its familiar pointed round fruit or seed.

As I walk my dog, we follow various routes, depending on his particular interest. My dog's name is Herb, and Herb has interests sometimes other than my

*Sailing ship captains carried cypress trunks in their ships for spare masts*

own. However, ideally, I try to follow a direction which roughly veers to the left as I cross the graveled road, pass the gum tree, some maples and ginkgoes, and move into a beautiful grove of stately pin oaks which are found frequently throughout the park. One of the features of Tower Grove Park that is constantly a surprise and a delight is to find groves of a particular species of trees, in considerable number and in various stages of development.

*Only three trees were on the land. Twenty thousand were planted.*

Turn slightly to the left and find a large oak tree which has a crown of branches, beginning about four feet above the ground and going in all directions. Take a sight, directly in line with the oak and a little to the north, to a gazebo of the nineteenth century, lovely and inviting, with its arched portals, louvered tower, and picnic benches scattered here and there. Now, look up and to the right, for directly in line with the gazebo is a magnificent pin oak, which must be the king of all pin oaks in the park. It is twelve feet, eight inches in circumference about three feet from the base. You must pause and drink in its beauty. It can be easily noted by its majestic branches and its height, as well as its circumference, as it rises from a clear small field, about a hundred yards in front of you. If, by chance, you do not find it, return to the junction of the path and the Walking Road, turn west on the Walking Road, and at the end of the first clearing on the right, you will see the mighty "King Oak."

Walk up to the gazebo. From this vantage point, in the Winter time, when the trees are bare, there appear a number of gazebo-like structures, and we could call this part of the park Gazeboland or the land of the picnic pavilions. All of the gazeboes have recently been repainted in beautiful colors, shades of gold, yellow, red, green, blue, rust and brown. But one of them, in fact, is not a picnic pavilion but a Music Stand. It is the large structure to the north and the right of the gazebo you are standing in. You will see more detail as we approach.

*Ten gazeboes were built in the park, based on European models.*

*The von Humboldt statue was unveiled with great ceremony in 1878.*

From the gazebo, crossing over to the traffic island, which is like a small oval park, walk into a grove of large poplar trees. One in particular will catch your fancy because of its unusual knotty trunk surface and grotesquely turned down limbs. In the Winter time it is a model for a gothic landscape. Towards the west, or on your left, at the beginning of the traffic island observe the large statue of Alexander von Humboldt, the famous German botanist who did extensive work in Brazil. At the base of the statue, on the south side, a bas-relief depicts Mount Chimborazo, the highest volcano in Ecuador, which he climbed.

Move now across the road on the other side of the traffic island away from the statue, toward another road and a small traffic island. By the side of the road is a row of ginkgo trees. We have passed specimens of this tree before, but this is a formal planting. The story of the ginkgo tree is an intriguing one. It is an ancient plant form, one of the first to propagate by seeds rather than spores. Its ancestors are millions of years old. Another name given to the ginkgo is the maidenhair tree, because its leaves resemble those of the maidenhair fern. Examine the interesting fan-shaped delicately scalloped leaves, which turn yellow almost overnight in the Fall, and color the ground with a golden blanket as they drop to the ground. There is a fruit from the female ginkgo tree which is rather foul smelling but which is gathered in the Orient for the edible seed which is considered a delicacy.

Crossing the little traffic island and the other road, approach the Music Stand, with its impressive marble red granite columns, topped by busts of several giants of the musical world. Some of their faces are a bit the worse for wear. But as you approach across the traffic island you will see, flanking the path, two who are well known, Beethoven and Wagner. Walk around the semi-circle toward the east to the other red granite columns and you will find two rather familiar figures, Mozart and Rossini. Stand there in the circle and enjoy the studied casualness of the little circular path coming off from your left as you face the street, and the more formal straight path leading to a small gazebo,

*Ginkgo Tree Leaves*

coming off a few feet to the right of the last path. Then look up into the Music Stand. Walk up the red cement sidewalk and drink in the beauty of the byzantine dome topped by a pointed decoration which looks very much like a Christmas tree steeple. Walk up the granite steps onto the floor of the Music Stand, and imagine sitting here a hundred years ago, with the bands that played the music, not only of Mozart and Beethoven, but also of John Phillip Sousa and whoever else you like best. On a Summer afternoon or evening you may still hear the music, some old, some new. As you face the towers with the concrete spheres on top, take the path toward the right, toward the two composers whom you have

*Shaw intended to add the busts of Sir Arthur Sullivan and Donizetti at the Music Stand.*
yet to meet, and make their acquaintance. They are the composers of opera, Gounod and Verdi, who grace this flank of the Music Stand. There is a vehicular road to our right now, and then beyond the park, Magnolia Street, where you can see many large old mansions. Continue on the path around the Music Stand toward the stone towers which are so characteristic of the various embellishments in this park, aptly named Tower Grove. Note the antique iron lamp posts, most of which do not presently hold lamps, on your right, behind the very large Osage orange trees.

*The "ruins" were constructed from stone debris of the Lindell Hotel, which burned in 1867.*
Beyond the two towers, continue on a path which leads to a red granite pedestal with a statue on it. To the left, out of the corner of your eye, is an alluring and attractive pond and ruins, which were built as a part of the mood of the park. Do not be tempted to follow there yet, because you will view them shortly in a very dramatic entrance.

You have now reached the small statue and can approach it and read the inscription. It says, "Erected to honor General Frederich Wilhelm von Steuben, in grateful recognition of his service to the American people in its struggle for liberty." This statue was contributed by the Steuben Society of America in 1968.

Leave the statue now and walk directly to the portal of the ruins facing the pond, through which you will see a lovely fountain. After lining up this view walk directly towards it. It is an impressive entrance to the artificial ruins of Tower Grove Park. The portals of the stone landing lead to steps which go down to the water. On a Spring or Summer day, or whenever the weather is warm, many small children will be found trying to scoop up fish, or dabbling in the water on the steps. After walking through the entrance turn around and look at the portals more closely. Walk on again around the ruins at your leisure and then take the little path leading off from the ruins, to the west. The path soon disappears into the greensward leading to the lily ponds. When the lilies are in bloom, from early Summer to late Fall or first frost, they present a beautiful sight. Walking around the semi-circular kidney shaped pools is a special treat for which you will want to provide time for your indulgence. Over the years I have seen these pools develop from simple holes in the ground to the rather permanent stone lined and formal pools that they are today. Some of the old pictures show lovely weeping willows overhanging the pools but the willows are no more. Walk around the pools. Note the bed of canna lilies over to the extreme west near the traffic circle and the picnic shelter or gazebo, on Center Cross Drive to the north, somewhat hidden by clumps of trees and bushes. It has a particularly interesting appearance if viewed some distance from the path toward the street.

*In 1975 the fountain was restored and lighted.*

*Water lilies were brought to the park by the first superintendent, James Gurney.*

If you go out to look at the gazebo more closely, glance to the north and you will see another ornate entrance to the park, with the typical towers, this time with a square base and round towers, topped by spheres of concrete. And also, a little farther in and set back, are two rectangular stone towers topped with statues of stags.

*The statues of stags were cast in Germany and weigh 700 pounds each.*

Walk back now along the path that circles around the pond, and as you look to the right you will see the traffic circle which has some interesting features, if you care to examine them. However, you must be careful in crossing the street here, because the traffic around the circle is blind and moving too fast to stop if you happen to be in the way of a vehicle. So, approach with caution if you decide to cross. Remember that traffic can be coming from several directions.

On the other side, in the center, is the magnificent elm tree, which is a landmark of the park. It is marked by a stone but the inscription plaque has been carried away. A few feet away from the elm, toward the large statue, stands a mulberry tree with a marker which was probably better constructed. On the marker are inscribed the words, "Mulberry tree planted on the spot marked by Adelaide Neilson, March 25,. 1880." This gives the venerable tree an age of around one hundred years.

Turn right around and be impressed by a magnificent granite base, topped by a statue of Shakespeare. In the polished granite pedestal we find plaques in relief of various characters from Shakespeare's plays: Lady MacBeth, Queen Katherine, and on the front the bas-relief of Falstaff as portrayed by a great Shakespearean actor of the later nineteenth century, Ben de Bar. On the north side we have a scene from Hamlet, the gravedigger scene, where Hamlet is holding the skull of Yorick, speaking to it, as the gravedigger looks on.

Now cross the street. Center Cross Drive, to the southeast, and you will be on the south side of Main Drive facing east. On the right is a tremendous picnic shelter, again with Byzantine styling, three enormous globe-like shapes topped by the interesting onion shaped ornament. The diameter of this picnic shelter is approximately seventy-five feet. It has a new roof, painted red and white and is a

*The "Turkish Pavilion" was first called "the pigeon or dove-cot summer house."*

favorite picnic ground for family reunions. This shelter, known as the "Turkish Pavilion," like all of the picnic shelters in the park, may be reserved by groups which make the proper arrangements with the park administration.

*The "Lodge" at Arsenal Street is now the administration office.*

After you have examined the largest circular picnic structure in the park, do not go to the Arsenal Street entrance, which is close and beckoning, but rather save it for another walk. Instead, walk leisurely through the woods there, towards the east, noting the various kinds of trees. There are too many to note here, but particular to this area is a large grove of pine trees of various sizes and shapes, each one with a rather unique trunk structure. A little toward the left is a simply magnificent specimen of oak with a development of branches that is very full and all embracing. Through the pines and oaks and elms, again cross the Walking Road, the same you crossed earlier. On the way is another view of a large picnic pavilion and in the center there is a gathering place for pigeons.

Now, relax, and indulge yourself for a few minutes, walking down the center of this nice wide gravel topped road, uncluttered by motor traffic, its quiet broken only by occasional inhabitants of the park, a person walking with a dog or sometimes a cyclist. On the right is a very interesting tree, knotty and gnarled. Along the gently curved road you will see a tree-lined bower composed of three linden trees with branches sweeping the ground, reminiscent of the romantic landscapes of Rousseau, or worthy of the brush of a Gainsborough. Now, where the road turns sharply to the left, it might be a good place, if you like, to cut out across the open field, or if you prefer, continue the walk along the tree-lined road.

*The gracefully curving "Walking Road" was once a wide carriage road.*

But, assuming you are cutting out across the field, you will walk by a large gum tree almost in the center of the field. Continue out to the center of the field. Look behind you, before you, to the west, and to the east, and savor the intricacies of the landscape design. The uncluttered field, gently uneven, not too studied in plane, broken here and there by lines of trees, set out from the road, leads one's eye to the sanctuary and silence of the tree-lined road which you have just left. The eye is taken here and there by the design of the landscaping, intricate patterns of continual interest.

*Pin Oak Tree Leaves*

Now, as you are in the center of the field, walking east, you come to a graveled path which you have not met before. You will see that on the left the path forks into a "Y" and if you wish now, you can leave the park by following the path to the right, where you will come out at Oak Hill Avenue. Or you can continue down the field, or the side of the park on the Walking Road, to the Roger Place entrance and exit there. All are equally pleasant. Herb and I prefer to continue down the field, drinking in the immense spaces which seem to refresh us in the crowded city, and enjoying the pleasure of the many species of trees which greet us all at once as our eyes rove around the landscape.

GRIFFON

89

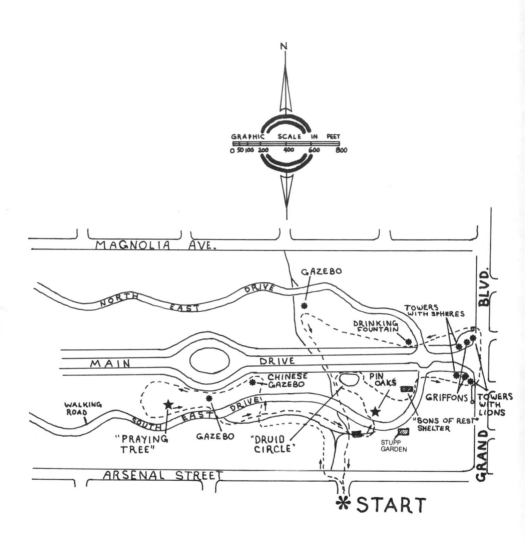

GRAPHIC SCALE IN FEET
0 50 100 200 400 600 800

MAGNOLIA AVE.

NORTH EAST DRIVE

GAZEBO

TOWERS WITH SPHERES

DRINKING FOUNTAIN

MAIN DRIVE

CHINESE GAZEBO

PIN OAKS

GRIFFONS

TOWERS WITH LIONS

WALKING ROAD

SOUTH EAST DRIVE

"PRAYING TREE"

GAZEBO

"DRUID CIRCLE"

"SONS OF REST" SHELTER

STUPP GARDEN

BLVD.

GRAND

ARSENAL STREET

＊START

- - - - - FOLLOW DASHED LINES FOR WALKS

*Walk 2 — The Eastern Area*

90

# The Second Walk

*"Many persons fail to see . . . the manifold points of interest in a finished park like Tower Grove because they only visit it when driving."*
David H. MacAdam, "Tower Grove Park", 1883

On this walk, choose a more formal entrance to Tower Grove Park. At Arsenal Street, just off Spring Avenue, is an impressive gothic, stone archway, with a stone up above, "1870." On either side is an ornate iron picket fence, flanked by low stone pillars with triangular caps. Stroll through the archway and notice the ornamental wrought iron gates. Continue a short way down a path flanked by park benches, to two short stone pillars, also capped by triangular stones. In the center, where the path divides, is a low stone marker, origin unknown. A path now goes to the left and to the right. Take the one to the left, over the slight rise. Where this path makes a sharp left turn, look to the right and see a gazebo, half hidden in the trees, except in bare Winter. Walk toward the gazebo, through a grove of pin oaks and past massive poplars on the right, to a ginkgo grove where you will find the Chinese gazebo with sheet metal sculptured dragons on the corners. Go through the gazebo and see a stand of maple trees, then turn immediately left and walk to a big old hackberry tree, close by a large oak. You may want to stop and read the many inscriptions on the venerable hackberry tree. Work your way over westward to a frail looking T-shaped gazebo with a brick floor. Admire its simple lines with cast iron scroll work across the top, some of which has been knocked off. Look across the road to the north and observe the gazebo's twin on the other side.

Continue walking west to a grove of four large hackberry trees, easily visible because of their smooth gray bark mottled with large scaly patches. Farther on is a grove of pin oak and poplar. Go right, or northwest, to the path by the road to a humped back bridge with iron work sides in the pattern of a circle enclosing a cross. There is also a stone canal and bridge on the right. On the left is another bridge crossing the Walking Road. Pause at the top of the humped-back bridge and take in the scene around. Turn left, toward Arsenal Street and walk toward the lattice work bridge. Cross below it where there is a mulberry tree with three trunks. Continue walking east, either through the woods or along the Walking Road. Along this road on the left you will see a small tree with arms outstretched to heaven, the "Praying Tree." Soon on the right you approach a paved path. Turn off on it, just past the T-shaped gazebo you passed going the other way. Follow the path until you spy a small stone bridge with a triangular cap, on the path, in the distance, then cut out across the woods to the stone bridge, and pick up the path at that point. Do not go to the large stone bridge on the main road.

Continuing on the path, cross the road into a little grove of pin oaks. Stand amid the pin oaks and then look north into the park, away from Arsenal Street, and you will *A carriage* see an opening in a circle of Osage orange trees, a druid *turn-around* circle of trees that seems to enclose a sacred place. *place may* *have been the* Standing in the group of pin oaks, walk directly toward the *origin of "the* opening in the grove of trees and imagine yourself in a druid *druid circle."* setting, where the priests are waiting and you come to participate in the ceremony. Note how regularly, though casually, the trees and overhanging protective bower are placed as if surrounding the scattered elm trees in the midst of the semi-circle. At certain times of the day there is a magic light filtered through the trees. Pause here for a moment or two for meditation or contemplation, taking yourself away from the cares of the day.

Go back now toward Arsenal Street and turn east on the Walking Road into the bend where you will see the Stupp Memorial Garden and Building, the latter a large structure with a copper-clad roof which resembles the gazeboes. On the Arsenal Street side an iron picket fence on a raised brick and stone foundation encloses a beautiful tree-lined garden with an entranceway of two brick pillars inscribed "South-Summer." Taking this path we walk into a flower-ringed fountain in the middle of which is a polished granite column. On top is perched a large bronze eagle with wings outstretched. The inscription around the fountain is "There is peace and beauty in a garden as the seasons come and go." It also proclaims, "Strength, courage and faith in the creator of the universe." At the bottom of the fountain a plaque tells us that it is "The Nicholson Fountain. In honor of David H. Nicholson, Member of the Board of Commissioners of Tower Grove Park."

*The Gurney family, James Sr., James Jr., and Bernice, administered the park for over 100 years.*

Continuing around the fountain we come into a semi-circular, stepped area with wooden slats that serve as benches, a kind of staging area for the Stupp Memorial Building. The roof is an octagonal structure, both upper and lower tiers. A plaque on the North Wall has the inscription "This Memorial Garden is dedicated to God and erected by Louise M. Stupp, in Memory of her parents Caroline and George Stupp and her brother Oscar C. Stupp, June 5, 1983."

The plaque on the West Wall is inscribed "The Stupp Memorial Garden, Tower Grove Park; Board of Commissioners: Robert J. Gaddy, President, Dennis G. Coleman, Carroll C. Gilpin, Gerhardt Kramer, Eldridge Lovelace, Peter Raven; Robert F. Denison, Park Director; Hellmuth, Obata and Kassbaum, Architects."

To the west of the building are eight picnic tables grouped together where outings for senior citizens are held. A little farther on you will see the added asphalt path that parallels Arsenal Street the whole length of the park. Across the street is St. John's Episcopal Church, a parish founded in 1841.

94

Go back now to the Walking Road where on the left is a large ornate picnic shelter, with gabled roofs running in two directions. This is the largest shelter in the park, known as "The Sons of Rest Shelter." Notice the ornate woodwork on both ends, and the intricately carved supports. You may want to take a minute now to inspect more closely the construction and art work of the wood in the gazebo. Note the little circles of wood, a progression of sizes, the columns on which the arches rest, the fine scroll work, the cut-outs of wood on wood, the rosettes which are brightly painted.

*Older persons walking along Grand Avenue often stopped at the "Sons of Rest Shelter."*

At the end of the road is a barrier, erected to discourage all but pedestrian traffic. On the right a rather large boulder marks a path, a formal path with concrete guttering, tree lined with low bushes. Follow this path, noting another tower, this time of different construction, with rectangular stone on stone, on a granite base. Take the main sidewalk now, walking past a row of gum trees surrounded by ivy. Approach the main gate from the inside to the outside and see two towers on the side gate, topped by spheres, and the beautifully ornate ironwork fence and gates. Walk through the gate to a concrete walk which leads to the right and see another high tower topped by a statue of a lion. Approach the iron grille work and inspect it more closely. Notice the fine artistic center work of crosses and circles, the lower crosses, the top scroll work, and, of course, the top of the posts, where there are very many ornate spindles of intricate design. All of this is on top of a low stone wall which is raised from the backdrop of the park, several feet, so that it frames the whole scene.

*The "weeping lions" are copied from statues on the tomb of Pope Clement XIII.*

Walk on the sidewalk to the street and then turn left, and now you can look back and enjoy, in one majestic view, the Grand Avenue or "East Gate" entrance to Tower Grove Park. The two central towers are topped by griffons.

*The griffon, a mythological beast, part lion and part eagle, kept watch over treasure.*

*View of Stupp Memorial Building*

Cross the park street, over the concrete traffic island. It contains a unique, though rather ugly, traffic lamp, one of the few traffice island lamps remaining in the city, which at one time boasted many at mid-street pedestrian crossings.

Walk past the street to the other walk and the tower with the statue of the weeping lion, and go back to the entrance, along the curving path. Again you have an opportunity to enjoy the beauty of the ironwork fence and stonework base, which is a scene of opulence and magnificence. Through the gate, then, the tree lined path appears in a new perspective, enclosing you, bringing you into contact with nature, the gum trees overhead, closing in, with ivy encircling them. On the right, behind a little gnarled tree, is the twin of the small tower passed on the other side of the road. In the small traffic circle is a statue of Christopher Columbus. You approach it, as you have most things in the park, from behind. Each year this statue is the site of a Columbus Day observance.

*In 1886 the first bronze statue of Columbus in the U.S. was unveiled in the park.*

Continue on down the path, crossing the street, which is a traffic street, and see the iron drinking fountain, which is usually bubbling all the time, attracting birds in all kinds of weather, as well as children. Far off on the right observe an impressive stone arch through which a path leads to Grand and Magnolia Avenues. You may leave the main path now or stay on it, walking west toward a gazebo which you will see on the right. As you move in that direction you will pass a very large tulip poplar which dwarfs the surrounding trees by its size and height. The octagonal gazebo, which is painted several perky shades of blue, is topped by a cupola and a globe, again with patterns of cut out wood on wood. Notice the scroll work and the wooden buttons on the arches which resemble the nineteenth century decorations of electric lights, so popular at the time when this was built. As you walk through one of the arches, you will note the brick floor, bordered by stone, and the pattern of the brick. It is unique in that each octagonal section is laid out from the center to the edge in a pie-shaped wedge divided by vertical bricks, reminiscent of a time when craftsmanship was valued more than today.

*A childrens' playground once stood next to the octagonal gazebo.*

*Poplar Tree Leaves*

Back from the gazebo, take the path across the main road and follow it to the entrance on Spring and Arsenal Streets where you came in. Along the path, notice the lovely stand of huge poplar trees on the right, and also, now, look back and regard the graceful gazebo which you have just visited, through the trees, across the road, in a new perspective.

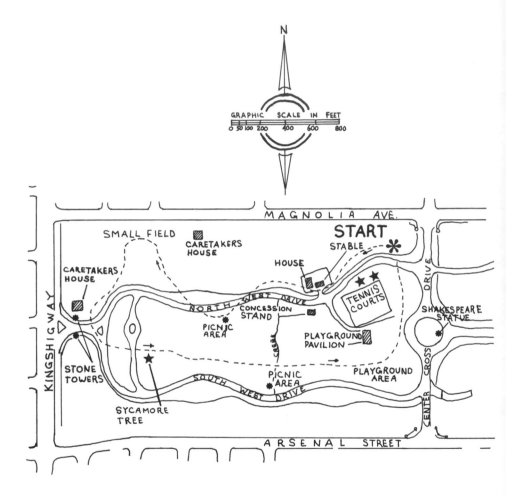

N

GRAPHIC SCALE IN FEET
0 50 100 200    400    600    800

MAGNOLIA AVE.

SMALL FIELD

CARETAKERS
HOUSE

**START**

STABLE

HOUSE

CARETAKERS
HOUSE

NORTH WEST DRIVE

CONCESSION
STAND

TENNIS
COURTS

SHAKESPEARE
STATUE

KINGSHIGWAY

PICNIC
AREA

CREEK

PLAYGROUND
PAVILION

STONE
TOWERS

SOUTH WEST DRIVE

PICNIC
AREA

PLAYGROUND
AREA

CENTER CROSS DRIVE

SYCAMORE
TREE

ARSENAL STREET

------- FOLLOW DASHED LINES FOR WALK

*Walk 3 — The Western Area*

98

# The Third Walk

*". . . citizens of St. Louis or visitors from abroad . . . should seek
occasion to view them without hurry. . . . To do this thoroughly
they can hardly avoid walking a part of the distance."*
*David H. MacAdam, "Tower Grove Park", 1883*

Near the statue of Shakespeare, west of the
traffic circle, are the tennis courts and the children's playground. The third walk begins here, on the path across from
the tennis courts' administration building, in front of which
stand two ivy covered trees. Across the street, on the north
side, are two giant poplar trees and beyond them two great
basswood trees. Over toward Magnolia Avenue you will see
a buff colored brick building which is the headquarters of
the National Council of State Garden Clubs. It is on a corner
of Shaw's Garden, another gift from Henry Shaw, one of St.
Louis' greatest benefactors.

*A bronze profile of Henry Shaw hangs in the tennis courts archway.*

Walking west down the shaded path come to a
stone maintenance building, which was once a stable. A
little triangular niche at the top looks as though it may have
held a bell at one time. Right before it is a caretaker's building, a house of stone, with a fence, iron gates, and two small
towers.

On the left is a concession stand, which is fairly
new and does not appear to go with anything else in the
park. But it is painted a subdued brownish gray, so that it
does not clash with anything.

*A plaque of the Gurney family hangs next to Shaw's.*

The gravel path here is interesting, curving,
meandering, toward the western entrance. Sometimes you
may want to stay on it and other times get off it. Your arrival
at the rear of the maintenance area lets you know that the

park is not the simple wooded sanctuary we would like to think it is, but is forever the creature of continuing maintenance, supply, death, and renewal, with mounds of gravel, salt for the roadways in Winter, and dead trees, their trunks lying abjectly on the ground.

The path continues to a small footbridge. It goes over a stone-walled drainage ditch. A little farther down, on the left, is a picnic pavilion. Cross the road and take a look at it. It is not a very large structure, but massive, with sixteen substantial stone columns supporting it. It is the only example of this type of picnic shelter in the park, and is probably of a later date than the gazeboes in the eastern part of the park.

At this point you may notice some of the smells of the area, the pungent fumes of what may be a smelter, and the smell of fresh baked bread. This end of the park, west of the tennis courts, is in striking contrast to the east end, principally because of the absence of gazeboes. One might speculate that this area was developed last, since the western end of the park did lie beyond the limits of the City of St. Louis when Henry Shaw made his donation of the land.

Now cross back over the road to the north side. There is a small field here of an intimate, human scale, a kind of clearing with trees around it, a very pretty spot. A little haze hangs over it on some mornings. The trees are nicely placed. There is a house in the park facing Magnolia Avenue. As you progress along the field, it narrows down to some embracing trees, and then opens up again, to an inviting little field about fifty or sixty feet wide, ending in a clump of trees down by the Kingshighway and Magnolia corner entrance.

Over a little farther south is a kind of wood dump, for wood chips, tree trunks, and branches piled high, rather secluded by little shrubs and evergreens. The traffic circle near the Kingshighway entrance includes a bed of canna lilies. It has a fence of heavy iron links around it supported by iron posts at low level which looks protective, though open on one side.

To the west is the caretaker's house, on the north of the Kingshighway entrance. Here you can see the entrance going out. Sneak up on it so as not to be overwhelmed by its formal majesty, but just let it be surprised by your capricious eye. You will see the castle-like towers of stone and iron gates which characterize the theme of the park. Across the street is the Holy Innocents Catholic church. Go back into the park through the entrance, toward the iron flower pot in the traffic island, to the canna lily bed. Beyond, toward the right, is a great sycamore.

*The "West Gate of King's Road" with towers forty feet high, once had iron gates with ornamental lamps.*

Looking to the east after crossing the little traffic island, there is an impressive vista. The field opens up very broadly with large trees on either side, and they seem to march into the field for a little distance, and then there are many trees in the far background, their black trunks being most prominent. At the very end there is a kind of a tunnel of boughs of trees, and out across there you can see another landscape up ahead. This is, to me, the epitome of the English landscaping art. There is often an early morning haze over the whole scene which adds a romantic touch to it.

*Henry Shaw created a strolling park, "a place of tranquility and ordered beauty."*

The smell of the bakery fills the air again. It might be the large chain store bakery on Spring Avenue, some blocks away, or, more likely, the flavor and extract company on nearby Kingshighway just south of Arsenal Street.

Now walk through that tunnel of green which was seen from a distance before, coming out into another field. It is a beautiful part of the park. Again, one of the intriguing things about the park is that you might see it in a different way each day. On warm and humid days the smell of the pines is strong.

Before you, discover the scene of a picnic area, small, with wide open spaces around it. On the South Drive there is a sign that says Picnic Area X, and this must be it. Walk a few yards to a square picnic table, about twenty feet on a side, which is constructed in one piece, with an opening on one corner. Actually, only two sides are about twenty feet long, and the other two sides, framing one of the corners, are about twelve feet long, leaving the corner opening, at which point is a stand-up bar-be-que grill. Though it is small, it probably could handle the crowd that the table might accommodate by cooking in several shifts. One might want to put another grill, brought from home, over the grill for cleanliness and to keep things from falling through the rather wide open spaces of the bars. The tables are pleasant enough, though. There are two of them, each under a large tree, on the edge of a bright green meadow that rolls down toward the west, with large trees nicely spaced nearby so that there is plenty of shade and sun, one towering cypress being quite impressive.

*The practical aspects of the park are represented in its playgrounds and playing fields.*

On the other side of a creek, which is grass covered and palatable to the eye, there is a concrete platform with several picnic tables arranged in two rows about twelve feet apart. The bar-be-que grill is several feet away from the table which will help to keep smoke away from the picnickers. There is a water standpipe close by, as well as a fountain bubbler. This is a very pretty scene, distinctively different in its arrangements, accommodations, and landscaping. Along the creek there is a line of young, white bark birch trees, with leaves that rustle in the slightest breeze, and bark that shines white in the sun. Not far away to the east are the tennis courts, children's playground and wading pool, all reached without crossing the street. It is a very pleasant picnic area for both youngsters and adults.

Continuing the walk, come up now behind the tennis courts, where there is a Greek style building, an open colonade with rest rooms at each end. Beyond it is a wading pool. There is a grove of pin oaks before the tennis courts and the playground. A fence encloses the tennis courts, and a tree bench is right outside it. By the playground is a magnificent oak tree. From here glance toward the Magnolia Street entrance and see the stag on the tower which you saw in the first walk.

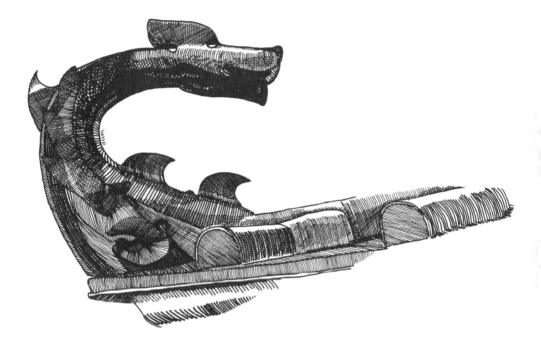

*The Dragon - detail, Chinese Gazebo*

ACKNOWLEDGEMENTS . . .

For wiping up dirty footprints in the hall after rainy day walks and other sundry chores—my wife,—"Dolly"

For drawings and maps—Dan Weismann

For editing—Mark Miller

For page decorations—Fred Houska and Dan Weismann

For reading and comments—Robert Denison, Sally Eaton, Bernice Gurney, Irma Tucker

For typing and proofreading—my daughter, Rita

For base maps—Board of Commissioners, Tower Grove Park

For historical notes—

Missouri Botanical Garden Bulletin, Vol. LXIV, August 1976, St. Louis, Mo.

Barbara Mykrantz, Archivist, Missouri Botanical Garden Library

Neighborhood News, May 23, 1946; July 25, 1946; August 1, 1946; September 5, 1946; October 30, 1947

St. Louis Globe-Democrat, August 23, 1939

St. Louis Post-Dispatch, January 16, 1920

St. Louis Star-Times, April 24, 1946

St. Louis Times, August 2, 1923

South Side Journal, August 10, 1949

Tower Grove Park, Facts in Capsule, mimeographed, n.d.

Tower Grove Park by David H. MacAdam, R.P. Studley & Co., 1883, St. Louis, Mo.

For translation into Braille—Don Charpiot and the Braille translators

For walking and talking—many friends, among them Mark, Dan, Pam, Fred, David, George, Emina, Geo, Rita, Pete, Ann and Bill.

This book was designed by Robert E. Knittel and Daniel J. Weismann with assistance from Patrick Murphy

The text type—11 point on 13 Helios

Margin notes type—7 point Helios italic

Headline type—24 point Windsor

Title type—Arnold Bocklin

The text paper is Artone ivory, seventy pounds